BOHÈME COOKING

BOHÈME COOKING

French Vegetarian Recipes

Carrie Solomon

Countryman Press

An Imprint of W. W. Norton & Company
Independent Publishers Since 1923

For information about permission to reproduce selections from this book, write to Permissions, Countryman Press, 500 Fifth Avenue, New York, NY 10110

For information about special discounts for bulk purchases, please contact W. W. Norton Special Sales at specialsales@wwnorton.com or 800-233-4830

Manufacturing through Imago
Book design by Studio Polka
Production manager: Devon Zahn

Countryman Press
www.countrymanpress.com

An imprint of W. W. Norton & Company, Inc.
500 Fifth Avenue, New York, NY 10110
www.wwnorton.com

978-1-68268-759-8

10 9 8 7 6 5 4 3 2 1

To Margie, Ellie, and Christoph

Contents

Introduction

I first moved to France on a whim about 20 years ago. I could say I did it in order to learn the language, although, really, I did it for the bread and cheese—a staple of my college vegetarian diet. But at the time it was far from *la belle vie* for a budget vegetarian in Paris. Restaurants were promoting nose-to-tail cooking, chefs had yet to start serving vegetables from their own gardens, lardons were scattered on every frisée salad, and the cheese plate ordered as a main course at the neighborhood *bistrot* was replied with a "*c'est tout?*" of thinly veiled sarcasm. This was well before the advent of natural wine bars and small plates of exquisitely curated vegetables. The vegetarian offering was quite slim and outsiders often wrote off French cooking as too restrained and exclusive. Nowadays, if you look at the menus of France's neo-*bistrots* or its most acclaimed Michelin-starred establishments, you'll notice that vegetables are no longer an afterthought or designated as a mere side dish. Whether oven-roasted inside a bed of sea salt, served cold in vinaigrette with fresh herbs, lightly brined in Normandy cider, or plated next to a harissa mayonnaise, vegetables are *en vogue*.

The trend isn't just in Parisian restaurants. Permaculture farming is on the tip of everyone's tongue, school children eat vegetarian meals twice a week, and in 2021, a small unassuming restaurant in the southwest of France became the first to receive Michelin stars for its entirely vegan menu.

But during my first months in Paris, I subsisted on Camembert and fresh baguettes. I got my exercise hiking up to the seventh floor apartment where, not having a place of my own (nor a kitchen of my own), I slept on a friend's couch. I blew my money on cookbooks and managed to crank out some decent dinner parties on my friend's old hot plate. As my savings began to run out, I even tried to convince myself of the merits of Hemingway's humble onion sandwich (à la *Down and Out in Paris and London*, a memoir by George Orwell). But there were limits to the magic of a crunchy baguette. I realized I needed my own place to cook.

The bucolic markets of Montmartre didn't make my kitchenless situation any easier. Temptation to get creative with food was everywhere. The season for figs that summer lasted well into late autumn, and the eggplants were so abundant that they fell off the market stands and rolled into the streets. But I had nowhere to cook them. With wishful thinking, I picked up a straw basket at a flea market, knowing that one day I'd bring it home filled with heaps of vegetables, and I'd get cooking.

Fed up with not having a place of my own, but with a small budget, I knew I'd have to find a roommate—at best. I copied a 10-digit number on a slip of paper, put on my best phone French, and a week later the kitchen of my dreams fell into my lap. It overlooked a flowered courtyard, had a serious gas range and parquet floors, and a gorgeous, mismatched collection of art deco plates—but it also came with a family of six.

Seated for my first Sunday lunch as the new au pair for a young French family, I marveled at the culinary bounty they ate from. The table was piled high with rosemary-steamed artichokes and cauliflower au gratin. Grandparents and cousins descended upon the apartment for the weekend meal. The older kids gave me a primer in French table etiquette: the salad leaves were to be folded, not cut. And the cheese must always be sliced in an equitable manner (if it was round it could be cut into even triangles, but if it was a large slice, then it must be cut from the center out, which creates equal portions, lest one hoard the best and most tender part for themselves). Bread was not to be put on the plate with your food. It either sat on its own plate or was placed directly on the table—this last one baffled me. Luckily the extended family only came for lunch once a week. The rest of the time, my role as an au pair was the definition of *bourgeois-bohème:* the kids had the right manners but unkempt hair, their mother wore a motorcycle jacket and they had a collection of vintage ashtrays—and although she often had a cigarette in her hand, she never lifted a finger in the kitchen. They lived in a former factory in the 11th arrondissement, and although the Sunday lunches were rather stiff, they took place over lots of wine on a four-meter-long glass dining room table, just below the parents' vertiginous loft bed. They didn't cater to their kids, didn't buy industrial foods, and were overall quite frugal. Produce only came from the affordable open air market, and what didn't fit in the fridge would decorate the counters or be heaped in a wooden wine crate by the door to greet visitors.

Soon enough I was in charge of simmering down the weekend ratatouille of eggplant, peppers, zucchini, and tomatoes. The French have always known how to coax maximum flavor out of vegetables, such as with this humble end-of-summer stew. I learned that ratatouille was forgiving when the tomatoes were a little too ripe, indulgent when topped with grated aged Comté, and chicly frugal when served the next day with poached eggs and croutons from leftover *pain de campagne*.

After a couple months, I was so comfortable in the kitchen (and in my new home) that I began hosting dinner parties when my adopted family was away for the weekend. As long as there were leftovers for their Sunday night dinner they didn't seem to mind. It was mostly cheap Côtes du Rhône and vegetable canapés on a budget with the occasional cheese soufflé, but when served with the shabby-chic flatware belonging to my bohème family, it managed to have a charming effect. I could still hardly speak conversational French, but my culinary vocabulary was expanding. Hervé, the children's father, gave me a huge copy of *The Escoffier Cookbook*. As I made my way through it, I was pleasantly surprised to find so many vegetarian recipes. Soon enough my host family began asking me to take care of dinner on nights when they would entertain guests; endives in béchamel sauce and winter vegetables with burgundy wine became mainstays that first winter.

Most Americans think of French food as rich, with a heavy use of butter, cream, and wine sauces. I will be honest, these do hold their place in French cooking, but it's all about balance: There are just as many recipes with light Dijon-based béchamels, vinaigrettes, and herb sauces. As I was juggling my new cooking responsibilities at home, I also started to find editorial gigs ranging from recipe testing to food styling and photography. Sometime after my first summer in the city, I started to hear about a chef who was said to be shaking up Paris's culinary landscape and maybe even that of the country itself. A chef who had entirely stopped serving red meat, completely transformed his menu, and put vegetables at the center of the plate.

The chef was Alain Passard, and his sea salt–crusted celery root was a three-waiter affair, served with pomp on gleaming steel platters and sliced tableside. He brought his vegetables in directly from his farm via the TGV high-speed train. The gardeners themselves delivered the wooden boxes of vegetables at the kitchen door every other day.

It intrigued the tony clientele of former presidents and actors, and the press swooned. Passard turned the tasting menu upside down: Vegetables were served to lavish effect, and only occasionally accompanied with small amounts of animal protein—almost like a mere afterthought. With some luck, I managed to get an assignment and my foot into the kitchen door at Arpège, Passard's three-starred Michelin institution on the rue de Varenne next to the Musée de Rodin in the city's seventh arrondissement.

Chefs from the world over would seek out apprenticeships in Paris's most acclaimed restaurants, and Arpège was considered la crème de la crème. Even though I wasn't apprenticing, I had come up with a book project that would get me access to the kitchen as well as the chef's vegetable garden about two hours from Paris. Although the book was never published, while in the kitchen of Arpège I saw how to caramelize beets and boil eggs five different ways. It was at Passard's vegetable garden where I first discovered Jerusalem artichokes and various root vegetables, and where he told me that some of his clients were reluctant to consider root vegetables worthy of white tablecloth dining. A staple of wartime food rations, and even known as legumes oubliés (forgotten vegetables), most French diners never expected to see them on a Michelin-starred restaurant menu. But Passard, who regularly told me that it was perfectly fine to eat with one's fingers, threw these notions of haute cuisine upside down.

For my first visit to Passard's garden, I was expecting a bucolic weekend in the country. I knew there was a château on the property, so I was looking forward to a respite from my frugal existence in Paris. But upon arrival I was surprised to find a crumbling half château, without heat or towels, and with only the bare basics. It was so cold the first night that I slept with socks on my hands. But in the early morning, as I came down the dark stairs, I was rewarded with apples roasted in the fireplace and locally churned butter. That weekend I tasted roast celery root and raw kohlrabi for the first time. For a vegetable that at the market had seemed far from noble, it took on new proportions when peeled and sliced by the right hands.

Eating Passard's vegetables became a rite of passage for those on the culinary food circuit in France, and above all it changed the way chefs serve vegetables in their restaurants. Gone was the token wilted spinach or green salad. Instead, entire menus with multiple odes to vegetables popped up not just in Paris but also in Lyon, Marseille, and Bordeaux. Food festivals were created that starred the chefs who had trained under Passard, and more chefs started growing their own greens. The apprentices soon took the helms of bistrots, wine bars, and restaurants across France. Whereas some people claim French cooking to be historically too mild, too sous vide, too old school, or too meaty— these chefs not only served more vegetables than their predecessors but were also less restrained in their approach. They served veggies whole, raw, or, shockingly, deep-fried (!) and alongside delicious brines, jus, and textured, spicy sauces. While true that some of these, like harissa, are the result of immigration from neighboring Mediterranean cultures with a deep and often complex history with the French (such as Morocco, Algeria, and Senegal), they have become essential to the flavor profile of French cooking and signal not only more inclusive cooking but also more expressive cooking.

In the years that followed my introduction to Passard's food, I married a Frenchman and had two children. Being pregnant in France was draconian torture—soft unpasteurized cheese tempted me at every dinner party, and it was hard to give up that evening glass of red. By the time my daughters were eating solid foods, life had taken on a more bourgeois tone. Meanwhile, our loft-like apartment slowly took on a more typical floor plan: walls went up to make bedrooms, proper closets replaced coat racks on wheels, and in the ever elusive search for more storage space in a city apartment, we even raised our bed a meter off the ground and slapped on a mini staircase to create what I called the basement. Even though the dining room pretty much disappeared with daughter number two, we still managed to hang on to a largish kitchen and a snug 10-person dinner table. We shared a nanny with our neighbor, and although I was reluctant to be away from my daughters, it was the only way I could get the time and space to write what would become my first cookbook for my French editor. From the door of our third-floor walk-up, our home looked quite ideal—the kitchen with the exposed beams, pots suspended from the ceiling-mounted rack I had always wanted, a bottle of wine in the decanter waiting for the kids to go to bed. But like an overloaded dishwasher, bitterness and the mental load chipped away at our flea market porcelain as well as our marriage. And when my daughters were two and four we found ourselves dividing up the appliances.

The years that followed were quite kid focused. I did find time to keep writing recipes though—mostly for French magazines or publishers—relentlessly pitching my editor at French *Elle* until I got a monthly recipe column. Writing recipes for French readers of the well-read women's magazine was a further lesson for me, not only on French cuisine but also on the French mindset—proudly terroir focused and less keen on ingredients shipped from the other side of the world. My editor would sometimes tell me to think about the readers who were different from me, those who didn't have access to niche ingredients or might be turned off by complex recipes or who lived in the countryside. This advice has guided me to create vegetarian recipes that are disarming and generous, indulgent yet balanced.

But as a single mom, and like all parents, I struggled to find balance, to eat healthy food, do a job I love, and still pay the rent. I've always been a night cooker, testing recipes at 11 PM, running the blender in a closet so as not to wake the kids. It was most often, in these moments, alone in my cramped and decidedly less bourgeois kitchen, that I made something new. It is here in my apartment in the third arrondissement that I learned not only to embrace but even to prefer an ad hoc, less-is-more lifestyle. It has brought me closer to the food I make and to the people I eat it with, because when you handle the rent on your own—the plates you put on the countertop for impromptu dinner parties taste even better.

A few years ago I met a handsome man who was born in Germany, raised in Belguim, and schooled in Italy—a real "Européen" as he will say himself. Even though my daughters have adopted him as their stepfather, we don't live together full time. He isn't a city person, so we go back and forth from Paris to the west part of France. It's only a two-hour ride in the TGV. In his home we built a small six-person dining table by hand. It doesn't get a lot of use, as I'm in Paris most of the time, but a dinner party usually beckons me there once a month.

Dinner conversations in France are often centered on food: where to shop, where to forage for mushrooms, how to choose persimmons. By virtue, the French are generous and adore sharing (even if their sharing often verges on showing-off) where they've found the best of this and that, a clever way to crisp up leeks, how to finish off a leftover bottle of red wine in risotto (page 182). Over the past 20 years I've been an exceptionally good

INTRODUCTION

INTRODUCTION

listener—whether at my ex-mother-in-law's Sunday lunch table, at the *fromagerie,* or while nosing around the kitchens of Parisian chefs. While I didn't go to Le Cordon Bleu, I did learn how to make harissa and pâte feuilletée. Through editorial assignments and apprenticeships, I rolled up my sleeves in many a Paris kitchen. In the last years I've been in more and more kitchens as a guest chef, resident chef, and consultant. I've created menus for restaurants and vegetarian recipes for the national school lunches. But what I always come back to, even more so when I'm cooking at home, is this relaxed vegetarian way of cooking.

In French you say "*se débrouiller,*" which means to find clever satisfaction with what is at hand. Whether it's serving up a last-minute meal at my kitchen counter (when a couple friends say they will "just come by for a drink" but end up staying all evening), or when I'm prepping a couple days in advance for a big Sunday lunch, I know that the most humble vegetable can be used to big effect. Spring onions can be quickly grilled and served over herbed yogurt with toasted nuts, just like celery root can be effortlessly grated into an ad hoc onion soup, all while staying unfussy and ungadget-y.

So don't worry if you can't find aged Comté cheese; it's all right—a decent white Cheddar will do, as will dried herbs when you can't get fresh. And for condiments like harissa and aioli, you can make your own (see pages 39 and 40, respectively). Most of the recipes in this book don't require fancy equipment beyond a vegetable peeler and box grater. And for the few recipes that do, if you don't have the equipment, just save the recipe for another time.

I'll take you through the basics of au gratin saucing and omelette making, helping you avoid pitfalls. I'll also help you make more whimsical recipes for condiments, such as Walnut Jam (page 44) and Mustard Seed Caviar (page 34). And for those occasions when you do want to show off a little in the kitchen, I'll guide you along as you stuff Corsican-style eggplants (page 143) or help you prepare a delightfully simplified mille-feuille (filo dough!) pastry (page 220). Whether you're trying to impress, or simply just trying to make a meal when your fridge is almost empty, I hope you will embrace this relaxed bohème way of cooking.

PANTRY

and Condiments

1

Homemade condiments are always hanging out on my countertop. It's where they have taken up their home because of their constant use. In my cramped Paris kitchen, it all happens at the counter: the chopping, prep, and, by default, a certain amount of storage. But I actually like to keep it all close at hand, just like my guests—making for an easy pour when my neighbor needs a refill on her wine or when the Charred Spring Onions (page 118) need some more Toasted Buckwheat (page 29) tossed on top. It's all at an arm's reach. Think of these recipes as little jars of redemption that come with just a shake or a spoonful. Condiments worthy of the small plates menu in a Paris wine bar and certainly your kitchen counter too. Most don't take more than 20 minutes active cooking time and will gift you spoonfuls of flavor ingenuity for days and even weeks to come.

If you're looking for advice as to what other ingredients to keep at hand in your fridge or cupboards, I'm more than keen on giving some. Aside from a halfway decent olive oil and some type of crunchy salt—fleur de sel being the obvious one for me—there are also a handful of ingredients I try to always have around:

- Briny things like capers, olives, and vinegars, as well as a lemon or two
- Toasted nuts and seeds for quick toppings that can also be tossed together last minute for an unexpected aperitif, or as it's known in France, *apéro*
- A couple kinds of mustard, ideally of varying textures and strengths
- A bunch of fresh herbs (although these can be kept in your fridge for longer life)
- Organic eggs, which I actually keep on the counter (it's a European thing)
- A little chili powder for last minute dusting—Piment d'Espelette (Espelette pepper) is just mild enough but has great effect, though local versions will do well too
- And finally, dairy—some sort of hard grateable cheese as well as something soft and creamy such as full-fat yogurt, spreadable goat cheese, or ricotta

XL Herbes de Provence

Makes: 1 to 2 cups (30-60 g), depending on bunch size
Preparation time: 2 hours, 5 minutes
Cooking time: 20 minutes

1 bunch thyme
1 bunch rosemary
1 bunch oregano
1 bunch sage
2 teaspoons sea salt, more to taste

OPTIONAL
½ bunch lavender flowers
½ bunch mint
2 tablespoons fennel seeds

Herbes de Provence should taste like the last whiff of countryside air as you begin your drive home to the city, slightly tinged with regret for not staying another night. Just before I leave my boyfriend's house in the west part of France, I run my fingers through the thick rosemary bushes that line the footpath to his house. When he comes to see me in Paris, he knows just what to bring: not flowers, but sprigs of fresh rosemary. This herb is the star, in my opinion, of herbes de Provence.

Unfortunately, most jars of commercially made herbes de Provence are quite uninspired, and they resemble more dust than herb, even in France. So that is why I make my own, coarse and crunchy, XL style blend. You can either make it all at once, if you have all of the herbs at hand, or make it little by little depending on what you get your hands on. If your neighbor gifts you some sage, great, dry it in the oven and stash it away in an airtight container. Do the same with a bouquet of rosemary and sprigs of thyme. There isn't an exact recipe, it depends on what you like. My herbes de Provence revolves around rosemary, thyme, sage, and oregano. I usually add smaller quantities of fennel seeds, mint, and lavender—or sometimes none of these. I suggest you don't grind your herbs, but rather gently crumble them in your fingers, leaving large or even XL pieces here and there. If you find you prefer different flavors than what I provide in this recipe, simply adjust it according to your preference.

1. Wash and pat dry all your herbs at least a couple hours before starting the recipe. Remove any tough stems from the herbs, or anything that might be unpleasant in your mouth. Preheat the oven to 325°F (160°C). Place all the herbs—including the lavender, mint, and fennel, if using—on a large baking sheet in a single layer and bake for 20 minutes. Take the herbs out of the oven, sprinkle with the sea salt, and allow them to cool.
2. Transfer the herbes de Provence to a large bowl and stir carefully with your hands, breaking up about one-third of the herbs as you go. Season to taste and add a little more sea salt if necessary. Store in an airtight container for 1 to 2 months.

NOTE: If you can't find one or two of the herbs fresh, follow the recipe as written with your fresh herbs and substitute any missing herbs for the dried version during the mixing stage. You might not get the same effect as making the whole recipe from scratch, but even if half the herbs start fresh your homemade herbes de Provence will already have a head start on many store-bought varieties.

BOHÈME COOKING

Fennel Hazelnut Dukkah

Makes: 1⅓ cups (165 g)
Preparation time: 5 minutes
Cooking time: 13 minutes

¾ cup (107 g) hazelnuts or almonds, with or without skin
4 tablespoon fennel seeds
1 tablespoon coriander seeds
1 teaspoon cumin seeds
¼ cup (36 g) sesame seeds
1 tablespoon sugar
1 teaspoon salt

This spice mix of Egyptian origin is my quick fix for giving almost any simple plate of vegetables a little added charm. Given the prevalence of toasted almonds and hazelnuts in *la cuisine française,* this crunchy condiment feels almost French. These days, dukkah seems to pop up on the menu of almost any self-respecting *bar à vin* or small plates joint whether you're in Paris or Marseille. On occasion, I completely omit the salt and double the sugar for a sweet dukkah that I serve with a generous amount of yogurt or even ice cream.

1. Heat the oven to 350°F (180°C).
2. Pour the hazelnuts, fennel seeds, coriander seeds, and cumin seeds on a dry, un-oiled baking sheet. Place the sesame seeds on a separate, dry, unoiled baking sheet. Place both sheets in the oven, the first baking sheet for 8 minutes and the second baking sheet for 5 minutes. Let cool. Set the sesame seeds aside and place the rest of the toasted nuts and seeds in a food processor along with the sugar and salt and blend until coarsely ground. Remove from the food processor and add the toasted sesame seeds. Store in an airtight container for up to 4 weeks.

NOTE: If you don't have a food processor, you can grind the nuts and seeds in a mortar and pestle. I have also used an immersion blender and a traditional blender with fair success.

Za'atar

Makes: ¼ cup (35 g)
Preparation time: 25 minutes
Cooking time: 36 minutes

1 tablespoon thyme, dried
  leaf, or 2 tablespoons freshly
  minced and then oven-dried
  (see steps)
1 tablespoon dried oregano
  or 2 tablespoons freshly
  minced and then oven dried
  (see steps)
1 tablespoon sesame seeds
½ tablespoon coriander,
  seeds or powder
1 tablespoon sumac
½ teaspoon salt

Za'atar may originate in Egypt, but almost all of its ingredients are native to France and found in French cooking, making it a great complement to our vegetables and grains, or a delicious dusting over a fresh cheese such as Corsican Brousse or ricotta. For extra texture, I sometimes toss it together with some lightly crushed XL Herbes de Provence (page 22).

Za'atar can have a coarser consistency, or you can make it finer by crushing it in a mortar and pestle or food processor. Using freshly dried and ground herbs—I suggest you follow the drying preparation in the recipe for XL Herbes de Provence—will give you maximum flavor. You can also use powdered herbs to good effect. There are many variations to this Egyptian-rooted condiment, so if you happen to be low on one, just add a little more of the rest.

1. Preheat the oven to 325°F (160°C).
2. If your thyme and oregano are fresh, wash and pat dry before starting the recipe. Remove any tough stems from the herbs, or anything that might be unpleasant in your mouth. Place the herbs on a large baking sheet in a single layer and bake for 20 minutes.
3. Spread the sesame seeds on a baking sheet and toast until just golden, about 10 minutes, and set aside. Spread the coriander seeds on a separate baking sheet and toast until just golden, about 6 minutes. Stir together (or grind in a mortar and pestle or food processor) the thyme, oregano, coriander, sumac, and salt. Add the toasted sesame seeds. Store in an airtight container at room temperature for up to 1 month.

Croutons and Herbed Bread Crumbs

Homemade croutons and bread crumbs are an effortless way to use up leftover bread and are so much better than store-bought. When I accumulate a few leftover pieces of baguette (or other types of breads) that are a day or two old, I often make croutons. If the bread is older than that and is too difficult to cut, I get out my food processor and make bread crumbs.

Croutons

Makes: 2 cups (80 g)
Preparation time: 10 minutes
Cooking time: 18 minutes

1 tablespoon melted butter
1 tablespoon sunflower or
  grapeseed or olive oil
¼ teaspoon minced garlic
¼ teaspoon salt
½ pound (227 g) bread, cut into
  cubes (approximately 2 cups)

1. Preheat the oven to 350°F (180°C). Stir together the butter and oil with the minced garlic and salt. Pour it over the cubed bread and using a spoon, or your hands, toss to thoroughly coat the bread. Spread the croutons on a baking sheet and bake until the edges are browned, 16 to 18 minutes. Let cool. Store in an airtight container at room temperature for up to 5 days.

Herbed Bread Crumbs

Makes: 1 cup (112 g)
Preparation time: 7 minutes
Cooking time: 14 minutes

½ pound (227 g) dry bread,
  cut into cubes (about
  2 cups), see Note
1½ tablespoons olive oil
3 tablespoon fresh herbs or
  1½ tablespoons dried herbs
  (rosemary, thyme, oregano)
¼ teaspoon minced garlic
1 teaspoon salt

1. Preheat the oven to 350°F (180°C). Place the cubed bread on a sheet pan and bake for 6 to 8 minutes, until the bread is quite dry. Transfer to a food processor and blend into coarse bread crumbs. Add the olive oil, herbs, garlic, and salt and process again for another 30 seconds, or until the herbs and garlic are combined with the bread crumbs. Spread the bread crumbs on a dry baking sheet and bake for 6 minutes. Let cool. Store in an airtight container at room temperature for up to 5 days.

NOTE: When making bread crumbs with especially dry bread, you might encounter difficulty getting the bread to break down. If so, place your bread in the oven at 350°F (180°C) for 5 minutes, let it cool for another 10 minutes, and then grind in the food processor.

Toasted Buckwheat

Makes: 1 cup (170 g)
Cooking time: 14 minutes

1 cup (170 g) buckwheat groats

I use this ingredient almost as I do croutons or bread crumbs. Buckwheat groats or seeds are perfect when you want something crunchy that doesn't contain gluten. Despite its name, buckwheat is free of wheat. It also makes for lightly fragrant tea when steeped in boiling water.

In France it's quite common to serve an herbal tea, or tisane, at the end of a meal, once the evening winds down and the last of the wine has been poured. It's also somewhat of a social cue to wind the evening down. I can only speak for myself, but it has been known to reduce the chance of a headache the morning after. One evening after a wine-fueled dinner, I realized I was out of tisane. I was pretty desperate to serve my guests something—it had been a long week and I didn't want the post-dinner conversation to go past midnight. Fearing my guests would stay all night, I pulled some toasted buckwheat off the shelf and steeped it in boiling water for five minutes. Thirty minutes later, although the sink was full of dishes, I was in bed.

1. Preheat the oven to 325°F (160°C). Spread the buckwheat evenly over a large baking sheet. Bake for 12 to 14 minutes until golden brown. Let the toasted buckwheat cool on the sheet. Store the toasted buckwheat in an airtight container for 1 to 2 months.

Tomato Confit

Makes: two 10-ounce
(280 g) jars
Preparation time: 20 minutes
Cooking time: 1½ hours

4 to 5 good-sized, ripe tomatoes
   (about 2 pounds; 907 g)
1 tablespoon olive oil
1 to 2 teaspoons thyme,
   fresh or dried
1 to 2 teaspoons rosemary,
   fresh or dried
1 teaspoon salt
1 teaspoon sugar

MARINADE (OPTIONAL)
1 to 1½ cups (200 to
   300 ml) olive oil
1 garlic clove
2 teaspoons herbs (thyme,
   rosemary, oregano, or herbes
   de Provence)
1 teaspoon salt

When summer gives you too many tomatoes, you can either make tomato sauce or confit tomatoes. If you're like me, too lazy for sterilizing jars and not interested in spending an August afternoon sweating over a pot of hot tomato sauce, then this is the recipe for you. Tomato confit is one of the most hands-off recipes I know, and it also makes one of the prettiest jars in your fridge. Serve them as they are, next to a bowl of olives, blend them into a Tomato and Goat Cheese Dip (page 63) or even smash them with the back of a fork over warm garlic bread.

1. Preheat the oven to 280°F (140°C). Wash and dry the tomatoes. Cut them in half or in quarters depending on the size. Place them skin side down on a very lightly oiled baking sheet. Drizzle with the olive oil and sprinkle with the thyme, rosemary, salt, and sugar. Place in the oven and cook for 1½ hours.
2. Once finished, remove from the oven and let cool. For drier tomatoes, leave them in the oven until completely cooled. Use the confit tomatoes right away or marinate them for up to 2 weeks in the refrigerator. To do the latter, stir the dried tomatoes together with all the ingredients of the marinade and store in an airtight container. The key for storing and ensuring freshness is to make sure that the olive oil completely covers the tomatoes.

Cornichons

Makes: 1 quart (1 L)
Preparation time: 10 minutes
Cooking time: 8 minutes
Rest time: 24 hours

1½ pounds (680 g) small
gherkins or cucumber spears

1½ cups (341 ml) white vinegar

3 cups (681 ml) water

1½ tablespoons
coriander seeds

2 tablespoons fresh or dried
tarragon, minced

1 tablespoon salt

1 cup (142 g) pearl onions,
halved, or sliced white onion

French style cornichons aren't sweet or garlicky or infused with dill like the pickles we know from elsewhere. They are made with small gherkins and rely on a salt brine with mustard seeds and tarragon. If you can't find fresh tarragon, you can used dried, or you can double the quantity of coriander seeds. And if you can't source small gherkins (as they are only available in early summer), you can replace them with cucumber spears.

1. Thoroughly wash the gherkins. Cut in half any that are much larger than the rest. Set the gherkins aside.
2. Add the vinegar, water, coriander seeds, tarragon, and salt to a medium pot and bring to a boil. Add the onions after 5 minutes, reduce to a simmer, and cook for 3 more minutes. Turn off the heat. Once the pickling liquid has cooled off so that it is warm but not hot (about 20 minutes), add the gherkins. Allow this to completely cool before transferring to an airtight container and placing in the refrigerator. The cornichons will be ready to eat in 24 hours. Store them in the refrigerator in the pickling liquid for up to 2 weeks.

Tomato Confit

PANTRY AND CONDIMENTS

Mustard Seed Caviar

Makes: one 10-ounce
(280 g) jar
Preparation time: 10 minutes
Cooking time: 1 hour

¼ cup (36 g) yellow
   mustard seeds
¾ cup (170 ml) white or apple
   cider vinegar
1½ cups (341 g) water
1 teaspoon salt
1 teaspoon sugar

These lightly pickled mustard seeds are another one of my favorite and simple ways to brighten up a plate of vegetables. Surprisingly similar in texture to caviar, these mustard seeds bring a little acidity and heat, without being overpowering. I like to add them to the Tomato and Polenta Tarte Tatin (page 155) or the Croissant Sandwich with Crispy Mushrooms and Béchamel (page 197). They also go especially well with other condiments such as capers, olives, Aioli (page 40), and all sorts of egg dishes.

1. Add the mustard seeds to a medium to large pot and fill with water. Bring to a boil for 10 minutes and then strain the mustard seeds, discarding the yellow-hued water. Fill up the pot again and repeat this process 4 to 5 more times, until the water isn't as yellow and the mustard seeds aren't too pungent. Place the mustard seeds back in the pot with the vinegar, water, salt, and sugar. Bring to a boil and then simmer for 15 minutes, until the liquid has reduced by about one-third. Keep the mustard seeds in their brine, refrigerated in an airtight jar for up to 4 weeks.

Le Pistou

Makes: ¾ cup (180 g)
Preparation time: 5 to
20 minutes

1 cup (54 g) fresh basil,
   lightly packed
4 tablespoons olive oil
2 tablespoons grated cheese
   (Parmesan, Comté, or
   Asiago), optional
⅔ teaspoon salt
½ teaspoon garlic

Pistou is a basil sauce common in *la cuisine niçoise,* which unabashedly draws its inspiration from neighboring Italy. But unlike pesto, pistou is made without pine nuts, and the cheese is optional. You can think of pistou as a lighter version of pesto. Traditionally, pistou is ground by hand in a mortar and pestle, which is quite practical if you're making a small amount. But I'm far from a purist, and unless I'm on vacation with extra time for pounding away at herbs, I usually double the quantity, especially if I'm making Pistou Stew with Seasonal Greens and White Beans (page 176) and quickly blend it up in my food processor or with an immersion blender.

1. Blend all the ingredients using a mortar and pestle, a food processor, or an immersion blender. Pistou can be somewhat coarse or fairly smooth, the texture is up to you. Store in an airtight container in the refrigerator for up to 3 days.

Mustard Seed Caviar

Ramp Leaf Oil (or Green Herb Oil)

Makes: 1½ cups (297 g)
Preparation time: 5 minutes

1 cup (30 g) ramps or wild garlic leaves, roughly chopped (you can also substitute dill, parsley, basil, or spring onion)
1⅓ cups (267 ml) olive or grapeseed oil
A pinch of sea salt

This verdant oil is an excellent way to get a little more use out of leftover green herbs, especially the leaves of some just-foraged ramps. Drizzle this oil over ricotta or fresh goat cheese with a handful of toasted seeds on top for an easily impressive crudités dip, or use it to brighten up almost any vegetable or vinaigrette. Ramps are really amazing, but you can also use dill, parsley, or spring onion greens—adding in a little fresh garlic clove if you like—to get a similar effect.

1. Rinse and dry the ramp leaves completely with a towel in order to avoid adding water to your oil. Add the ramps, oil, and salt to a blender or a handheld mixer and blend for 1 minute. Pour the mixture into cheesecloth and filter completely into an airtight container or glass jar. Keep refrigerated for up to 2 weeks.

NOTE: Once you strain the oil, you can keep the remaining cream and use it as you would a pesto, adding in a little shaved Parmesan and ground pine nuts.

Red Pepper Harissa

Makes: ⅔ cup (150 g)
Preparation time: 10 minutes
Cooking time: 1 hour

3 red bell peppers
1 medium red chile pepper
   (such as Anaheim or
   Fresno), see Note
5 tablespoons olive oil
1 teaspoon salt
¼ cup (56 ml) cider or white
   wine vinegar
½ garlic clove
1 teaspoon cumin powder
1 teaspoon coriander powder
1 teaspoon caraway seeds
½ teaspoon smoked paprika
½ teaspoon sugar

This deeply flavored hot sauce can be made in varying intensities. The red bell peppers provide a base from which you can create a mild sauce or one with more strength. The same goes for the garlic. If you'd like more than the recipe calls for, don't hesitate! While commonly served with North African dishes, I also like to add harissa to soups, serve it as a dipping sauce for Panisse Chickpea Flour Frites (page 84), or blend it with Mayonnaise (page 40) to make a Spicy Egg Salad (page 203) that is perfect on a baguette.

1. Preheat the oven to 325°F (160°C). Cut the red bell and chile peppers in quarters and clean out the seeds. Place the quartered peppers on a baking sheet and drizzle them with 1 tablespoon of the olive oil, sprinkle with salt, and place in the oven for 1 hour. The edges should be slightly blackened—making them easier to peel. Once the peppers have cooled completely, peel, and discard the skin. Place the red peppers and the rest of your ingredients in a food processor or blender and blend until smooth. I prefer using a blender, as the sauce will be the smoothest, but you can adjust according to your preference.

NOTE: The amount of chile pepper you add to your harissa will change the intensity of the spice. If you prefer a mild harissa, add less chile pepper. If you prefer more spice, add more. Sometimes within the same variety, heat will vary greatly from one pepper to the next. I usually add the pepper little by little, tasting each time I mix and adding a little more to find the right intensity for me.

Mayonnaise and Aioli

Makes: 1⅓ cups (300 g)
Preparation time: 10 minutes

1 medium egg, organic,
  room temperature
1 tablespoon lemon juice or
  vinegar (ideally white vinegar,
  cider vinegar, or white wine
  vinegar), room temperature
1 teaspoon salt
1 garlic clove, minced, to
  make aioli
1 cup (198 ml) vegetable oil
  (grapeseed, canola, safflower,
  or sunflower)
1 to 2 teaspoons Dijon
  mustard, optional

The following two methods, which both use an entire egg, make for a rather light mayonnaise. Use the freshest organic eggs available and make sure that all the ingredients are at room temperature prior to making this recipe. Once you have gotten the hang of the recipe, and especially the method of emulsifying, don't hesitate to add additional flavoring (harissa paste, ginger, or a clove of minced garlic for aioli), but only once the mayonnaise has completely emulsified.

For some recipes like sandwiches, you may want to use a more compact mayonnaise, but for other recipes like Oeufs Mayonnaise with Fried Capers (page 79), I like a slightly more liquid mayonnaise. In the former case, you can create a denser, yellower mayonnaise using only egg yolks (see Note). In the latter case, I add 1 to 2 tablespoons of water at the end of the emulsification.

I tend to stay away from olive oil when preparing the base of a mayonnaise, but sometimes I do like to blend in a tablespoon or so at the end to increase the flavor without it being overwhelming. Occasionally, I will also finish with a nut oil such as sesame or walnut. For a verdant, herbaceous twist, I'll blend in some Ramp Leaf Oil (page 36).

METHOD 1 (IMMERSION BLENDER)

1. Crack the egg into the tall cylindrical container that is often sold with immersion blenders. You can also use a jar or other narrow container, but it should not be much wider (up to 3 inches; 8 cm) than the blender head itself. Add the lemon juice or vinegar, salt, and the minced garlic (if you're making aioli). Pour in the vegetable oil and let stand for 30 seconds. Place the immersion blender in the container, with the base flat against the bottom of the container. Begin blending on high speed, making sure the base stays firmly placed against the bottom of the container.

2. As the mayonnaise begins to form, in a small movement, gently lift one side of the blender base away from the bottom of the container, about ½ inch (1 cm), while leaving the other side touching the bottom. Repeat this movement to increase the flow of oil to the bottom of the container. Once 75 percent of the mayonnaise has been blended, lift the immersion blender higher to blend the remaining oil that remains on the surface. Blend in the mustard, if using.

METHOD 2 (FOOD PROCESSOR, ELECTRIC BEATERS, STAND MIXER, OR BY HAND)

1. Place the egg and salt in a food processor or in the bottom of a medium bowl adapted for electric beaters or a stand mixer. You want the bowl to be fairly deep in order to avoid being splashed by the oil, so don't use a small individual soup bowl. Think more medium salad bowl.

2. Process, beat, or whisk the egg for 30 seconds. Add the lemon juice or vinegar and whisk again until absorbed. Begin adding the oil in drops, blending or whisking to emulsify between each addition. Once you have emulsified over half of the oil into the egg, slowly begin to add larger quantities. Once the oil is completely emulsified, 5 to 15 minutes depending on your equipment, add the mustard, if using, and emulsify until smooth.

NOTE: If you want to make only egg yolk mayonnaise with an immersion blender, food processor, or stand mixer, you will likely need to double the quantities of every ingredient and follow the recipe above, using only egg yolks instead of full eggs. The reason for this is that the egg must make significant contact with the blade or whisk—if you don't have enough liquid egg matter in the bottom of your container, the mayonnaise won't emulsify properly with the oil and will then break. The exception to this is if you are whisking by hand, in which case, feel free to follow the recipe without doubling.

Dijon Mustard Vinaigrette

Makes: ⅔ cup (160 ml)
Preparation time: 5 minutes

1 tablespoon Dijon mustard

1 tablespoon
   stone-ground mustard

½ cup (100 ml) olive oil

3 to 4 tablespoons vinegar
   (cider, champagne, red or
   white wine, balsamic)

1 teaspoon salt

1 tablespoon sesame seeds

1 tablespoon minced
   shallot, optional

1 teaspoon crushed XL
   Herbes de Provence
   (page 22), optional

1 teaspoon fresh minced herbs
   (parsley, basil, thyme), optional

½ teaspoon fresh cracked
   black pepper

1 teaspoon freshly grated ginger

The first five ingredients of this recipe are an outline for a typical French vinaigrette—where you go from there is up to you. I often vary the type of vinegar I use, sometimes using several types in the same recipe. Depending on what I am making, I will also toss in some herbs or oils—I add a good spoonful of grated ginger and sesame oil when making the Haricots Verts and Herb Salad with Walnut-Ginger Vinaigrette (page 109), and I use walnut oil when making the vinaigrette for the Endive, Apple, and Roquefort Salad (page 99). If you like a slightly sweeter vinaigrette or if you find your mustard a little too bracing, feel free to blend in a teaspoon of honey. Tahini (sesame seed paste) also emulsifies well and is a good substitute for mustard. Sesame seeds can give added texture. If you're shy about using large quantities of olive oil, you can make a low-oil or even oil-free version of this recipe by using water and soy sauce in place of the oil, or even half yogurt for a creamy version. In my kitchen, no two vinaigrettes are ever the same.

TRADITIONAL METHOD

1. Place the two mustards in a small bowl. Stir in a teaspoon of the olive oil until emulsified and smooth. Stir in another teaspoon of olive oil and repeat the process until all the oil is added. Incorporate the vinegar teaspoon by teaspoon, stirring in between so as not to break the vinaigrette. Add the rest of the ingredients and stir well. Store refrigerated in an airtight container for up to 5 days.

BLENDER METHOD

1. Blend all the ingredients together with a blender or immersion blender. Store refrigerated in an airtight container for up to 5 days.

Walnut Jam

Makes: 1½ cups (480 g)
Preparation time: 5 minutes
Cooking time: 8 minutes

1 cup (128 g) walnuts
½ cup (50 g) shredded
   Parmesan cheese or other
   hard white cheese
¼ cup (50 ml) olive oil
1 tablespoon walnut oil
1 tablespoon vinegar
½ teaspoon salt
⅛ teaspoon garlic

This nutty jam goes well alongside a cheese plate, spread inside a croque monsieur, or stirred in a Creamy Pumpkin Polenta with Walnut Jam (page 146). You can also make it with pine nuts, cashews, and/or a mix of other tender nuts.

1. Preheat the oven to 325°F (160°C). Evenly spread the walnuts on a sheet pan and toast them in the oven for 8 minutes. Remove the walnuts from the oven and allow them to cool.
2. Once the walnuts have cooled, place them in a food processor with the rest of the ingredients. Pulse until the mixture is relatively smooth. Store in an airtight container in the refrigerator for up to 5 days.

Lemon-Herb Yogurt Remoulade

Makes: 1 cup (320 g)
Preparation time: 5 minutes

2 tablespoons capers, minced
3 tablespoons mixed minced
   herbs (dill, tarragon, chives,
   parsley, basil)
4 tablespoons Greek yogurt
2 tablespoons minced dill
   pickles or Cornichons
   (page 31)
2 tablespoons Mayonnaise
   (page 40) or store-bought
2 tablespoons lemon juice
1 tablespoon minced
   white onion
¼ to ½ teaspoon minced garlic
Zest from ½ lemon
Sea salt to taste

This remoulade is a zesty complement to a simple platter of vegetable crudités, or as a flavorful mayo replacement when spread inside a sandwich. It also brings crunch to the delicate flavor of Tempura-Fried Squash Blossoms (page 75). Remoulade is traditionally made with a mayonnaise base, but this lighter recipe adds Greek yogurt.

1. Mix all the remoulade ingredients together and salt to taste. Reserve in the refrigerator. Remoulade keeps for up to 4 days and in my opinion, usually seems to get better with time, so don't hesitate to make it ahead.

Homemade Salted Butter with Crunchy Fleur de Sel

Makes: ½ cup (113 g) butter
Preparation time: 15 minutes

2½ cups (568 ml) heavy cream
1 to 2 teaspoons fleur de sel or
   Maldon salt

Most French chefs tend to cook with unsalted butter because it makes it easier to control the saltiness of a recipe to their liking. You can, of course, cook with salted butter, but just bear in mind that you'll want to use less salt overall when seasoning your dish. In my opinion, salted butter is best when it's spread or used to finish a dish. And I think the best salted butters in France are made with flaky fleur de sel. While you can find salted butters outside of France, they never have the same crunch as a butter churned with fleur de sel, a special sea salt. Yes, I know outside of France you'll pay quite a lot for fleur de sel, so if you can't find it, or if it's too expensive, then I suggest Maldon salt, which is pretty close. Or, the next time you or someone you know goes to France, ask them to bring you back a pot of fleur de sel so you can make the perfect salted butter at home.

There are two options for making your own salted butter. The first option is to soften some high-quality butter (leave it room temperature for 1 to 2 hours) and blend in crunchy fleur de sel. Ideally, good butter should have a yellowish hue to it, as it indicates that the cows had ample time to graze upon grass and flowers. The second option is my preferred method, though it takes a little more *huile de coude,* or elbow grease. Here, 10 minutes and a stand mixer will turn heavy cream into the perfect spread.

Fleur de sel, which is gathered by hand in the coastal towns of Guérande and Noirmoutier, is collected by channeling sea water onto flat plains. Evaporation leaves large delicate crystals behind. It is by far the best salt to splurge on. Its delicate crunch makes it more like a condiment than a simple salt. Maybe this as a bit of a reach, but when I see the sparkling crystals on top of a plate of asparagus or whatever might be on the table, somehow it seems instantly more French.

1. Pour the heavy cream into the bowl of your stand mixer. Using the whisk attachment, begin to beat the butter on the lowest speed for 1 minute. Increase the speed over the next minute to the highest setting. The cream will quickly become whipped cream. Place the splash guard on your bowl at this point; if not, you'll end up painting your kitchen. Keep on beating until the cream begins to separate. Stop the stand mixer and scrape down the sides and then continue to beat until the butter clings to the whisk, about 10 minutes.
2. Remove the butter from the bowl and filter out the buttermilk. I like to use a nut milk bag, but you can also use standard cheesecloth.
3. Prepare an ice bath. Dip the butter into the ice bath and rinse off any remaining buttermilk. If the buttermilk stays on your butter, it will cause it to spoil, so rinse it well. Place the butter in a bowl and stir in the fleur de sel with a spoon. Mold the butter if you like or simply place it in a small airtight container in the refrigerator. I never end up keeping this butter for more than a couple days, as it makes everything taste better.

Marinated Labneh Balls

Makes: 12 ounces (340 g),
10 to 12 balls
Preparation time: 20 minutes
Rest time: 48 hours

1 pound (454 g) full-fat Greek
    yogurt 10%
2 teaspoons salt
Olive oil, optional

Labneh is more or less a soft cheese made with strained yogurt used in Middle Eastern cooking. While labneh isn't traditionally French, it speaks to the love the French have for all dairy, whether it's cheese, yogurt, or yogurt-based dips for serving at apéro hour. The latter are unquestionably similar to labneh. The labneh from this recipe can either be spread like a cream cheese (without all the stabilizers and artificial ingredients) or rolled into satisfyingly presentable little balls. And don't hesitate to take it a step further and add in seeds or minced herbs.

1. Drain any excess liquid from the Greek yogurt, then stir in the salt. Line a colander with two layers of cheesecloth. Place the salted yogurt in the strainer and close the cheesecloth around it, tying a knot with a string or rubber band. Place the strainer on a deep plate and put it in the refrigerator for 48 hours. Check on the yogurt and drain any excess liquid on the plate regularly.

2. After 48 hours, the labneh can be used immediately or formed into small 1-ounce balls (about the size of a ping-pong ball). For denser balls, strain for an additional 24 hours. Store the labneh in an airtight container. If you have made the balls, you can cover them with a little olive oil so that they do not stick together. Store the labneh for 3 days, or up to 1 week if you've covered it with oil.

APERITIF

or Apéro Hour

2

Apéro, as it's commonly called in France, is a convivial predinner drink that can often blur the line with *le dîner,* especially if there aren't solid dinner plans to follow. That being said, the timing of an apéro can be flexible, especially during holidays or over long weekends, when it can even make an appearance before a late lunch. Apéro is more or less an excuse to begin just a little earlier, to stretch out the pleasure, or quite simply to tide over hungry kids (or adults) before *le dîner* hits the table, which is usually around 8 PM for us. But apéro can also be a sort of meal, even a dinner on its own, an *apéro dinatoire,* or a small ceremony of appetizer-sized plates that allows everyone to linger over the kitchen counter or on the living room sofa, in lieu of a seated dinner. It takes the pressure off of deciding on only one main dish, and at my home, where I don't have a bona fide dinner table, this is pretty much my standard.

Whether as a stand-in for dinner, or a simple snack consisting of toasted almonds and cherry tomatoes, an apéro can take on many forms and sizes. France has a whole host of predinner drinks, ranging from licorice-tinged Pastis and regional bitter cordials to light wines like rosé. But you could also consider sparkling water. And why not a bottle of juice for the kids?

There are a few essentials: a tray for a few glasses, a bottle opener, and a couple bowls or small plates. From there, you might want to add cocktail napkins, ice cubes, and toothpicks—if serving olives or something cured in brine or oil. As a rule, the presentation should be slightly soigné, meaning given care. Therefore, an apéro should never be served out of plastic containers, and industrial soft drinks are shunned. Apéro can be served inside or outside, year-round. And while primarily a salty affair, I try to have some seasonal crudités such as radishes, cucumber slices, or carrot sticks on hand as well.

For me, apéro doesn't need forks or knives. As for the dishes themselves, there is usually a trio: crudités, something homemade, and some type of nut. In a pinch, roast peanuts will do, but don't shy away from toasting hazelnuts, cashews, and almonds yourself. In this chapter, homemade can mean something as simple as a Black Olive and Fig Tapenade (page 55) slathered on toast, or it can take on more elaborate forms, such as Tempura-Fried Squash Blossoms (page 75) or Red Pepper Tartinade (page 61). And don't hesitate to flip back to the condiment chapter for a little bowl of Cornichons (page 31) or Buckwheat Chips (page 67) for dipping—very apropos accompaniments.

Caper and Herb Dipping Sauce

Serves: 4
Preparation time: 5 minutes

6 tablespoons olive oil
1 to 2 tablespoons mustard
2 tablespoons capers, minced
1 tablespoon caper brine
1 tablespoon shallot, minced
2 tablespoons fresh herbs,
  minced
1 teaspoon dried herbs (thyme,
  oregano, or others)
4 tablespoons yogurt (full-
  fat, Greek or other thick
  variety), optional
2 tablespoons lemon juice
2 tablespoons vinegar
Salt
Pepper

I often make a thick, almost chunky vinaigrette-like sauce for serving with artichokes, steamed vegetables, or even moonlighting as a dip for crudités. I always start with a mustard and oil base, usually olive or grapeseed oil, but sometimes I will cut that with a good drizzle of walnut oil or sesame oil. Then I toss in whatever vinegary and briny condiments I have inside the door of the *réfrigérateur;* capers are a must, minced Cornichons (page 31) or pickles, a little horseradish, some Dijon mustard, and sometimes even stone-ground too, chopped herbs such as dill, chives, basil, oregano, a little spring onion and shallots, and dried thyme. When I'm feeling fancy I might drizzle in some smoked olive oil, mirin, or yuzu kosho. And for a creamy take, I often add a spoon of yogurt or crème fraîche (but sour cream will do just fine). Once I get a nice thick texture, I begin loosening it up with lemon juice, caper brine, and vinegar. For vinegar, I like cider vinegar, red wine vinegar, rice vinegar, and champagne vinegar . . . it all depends what I've got at hand. As a result, this sauce is rarely ever the same twice, and that's just fine!

I also use this sauce as a wonderful dip for vegetables that are good for scooping, such as artichoke leaves. Belgian endive leaves, or slices of black radish or daikon. If I'm not using this as a dipping sauce, I like it over steamed broccoli or cauliflower.

1. Whisk together the olive oil and the mustard until it emulsifies. Add the rest of the ingredients, in order, stirring between each addition. Season to taste. You can also emulsify the dipping sauce in its entirety in a food processor, just make sure to pulse little by little in order to avoid overmixing.

Black Olive and Fig Tapenade

Makes: 1¾ cup (437 g)
Preparation time: 10 minutes
Soaking time: 45 minutes

¼ pound (113 g) dried figs
8 ounces (227 g) black
  olives, pitted
4 tablespoons olive oil
2 tablespoons balsamic or red
  wine vinegar
1 lemon, juiced
1 garlic clove, minced
Salt

Tapenade is most often made with capers and anchovies, making it a very salty affair that's well-suited for serving with predinner drinks. This version is a little lighter, and less salty, but still worthy of aperitif hour. Try it spread inside of Flute Crackers with Cheese and Seeds (page 70), or simply serve it with sliced fennel for dipping. The slight sweetness of the figs also goes well with cheese, so don't hesitate to serve it on a toasted baguette with goat cheese. A tray of these makes for an especially beautiful addition to the table, especially if you top them with a little bit of Mustard Seed Caviar (page 34) and some fresh herbs or crispy fried rosemary (see Tomato Carpaccio with Crispy Chickpeas, Stracciatella, and Fried Rosemary on page 107).

1. Soak the figs in hot water until softened, about 45 minutes. Place them in a food processor along with the rest of the ingredients and blend until it's as smooth as you would like. Salt to taste. Store in the refrigerator in an airtight container for up to 3 days.

Green Olive Tapenade

Makes: 1 cup (250 g)
Preparation time: 5 minutes

1½ cups (213 g) green olives
2 tablespoons capers
2 tablespoons olive oil
1 tablespoon white onion or
   scallion, minced

This is one of those condiments that is good slathered on anything bread- or cracker-like (obviously!). But it goes with so much else as well: sunny-side-up eggs, spread on toast, a dip for carrots . . . I even use this tapenade as a dry marinade for Roast Cauliflower with Green Olive Tapenade (page 116). Occasionally, I blend in an additional ⅓ cup of blanched peas and a few basil leaves and call it an olive pesto sauce worthy of pasta! This recipe is truly a hybrid, a humble spread that can hold its own with a glass of wine at apéro hour or as a clever addition to many a recipe.

1. Place all the ingredients in a food processor and blend until it's as smooth as you would like. Store in the refrigerator, in an airtight container for up to 5 days.

BOHÈME COOKING

Red Pepper Tartinade

Serves: 4

Preparation time: 10 minutes

Cooking time: 1 hour
30 minutes

2 to 3 medium (2 pounds; 1 kg)
   red bell peppers

1 tablespoon olive oil, plus some
   for serving

1 teaspoon salt

3 sprigs oregano, optional

½ cup (114 g) Greek yogurt

7 ounces (200 g) feta or
   goat cheese

1 teaspoon smoked paprika

½ teaspoon Espelette pepper or
   chili powder, optional

2 tablespoons chopped
   olives, optional

Sea salt for serving

A tartinade is more or less the French equivalent of a dip, and the word literally means "to spread." With this recipe, you can both dip and spread. I usually double the quantity, as it goes with so much—vegetable crudités, Buckwheat Chips (page 67), spooned under a Tomato Carpaccio (page 107). . . . Sometimes I even spread it inside an egg sandwich or a savory Buckwheat Galette (page 204). Don't hesitate to make this a day or two ahead, as the flavors get even better.

1. Preheat the oven to 325°F (160°C). Cut the red peppers in quarters, clean out the seeds, and place the pepper slices on a baking sheet. Drizzle with the olive oil, sprinkle with the salt, and place in the oven for 1½ hours. Let cool.

2. If using the oregano, heat a small pan over medium heat and dry toast the oregano for 2 minutes, stirring frequently. Set aside for the topping.

3. Peel the peppers, discarding the skin. Place the peppers in a food processor, or use an immersion blender, and add the yogurt, feta, paprika, and Espelette pepper, if using. Blend until the mixture is smooth, 2 to 3 minutes. Pour the dip into a shallow plate and top with the toasted oregano, olives, if using, and a drizzle of olive oil and sprinkle with sea salt to serve, or store it in an airtight container in the refrigerator for 3 to 4 days.

Seasonal Tzatziki

Makes: 2 cups (454 g)
Preparation time: 15 minutes

½ pound (227 g) kohlrabi or
    celery root, zucchini, cucumber
1 cup (227 g) Greek yogurt, full
    fat is best (see Note)
2 tablespoons dill, minced, plus
    more to taste
2 tablespoons mint, minced,
    plus more to taste
1 to 2 garlic cloves, minced
2 tablespoons lemon juice
½ teaspoon sea salt, plus
    more to taste
Extra virgin olive oil to serve
Freshly ground black
    pepper to taste

I like to take the basic elements of a tzatziki recipe (yogurt, herbs, garlic) and vary them with vegetables that are in season. Fresh herbs are best, but dried herbs will work in a pinch, although you'll have to use a little more of each. The only firm criteria for this recipe is that the vegetables must be grateable. In the winter I use celery root, and in the spring I like to use radish or kohlrabi or even a handful of fresh peas (okay, actually I don't grate those; I chop them or run them through a food processor or blender). In the summer I sometimes use bell peppers or zucchini instead of cucumber. Just make sure you always thoroughly dry and remove any excess water from the vegetables you are using. This tzatziki is a delicious essential in Potato Salad with Tzatziki and Fennel (page 149).

1. Carefully peel the kohlrabi and grate it on the smallest grade of a four-sided grater. If necessary, you could also use a small hand grater or food processor. Place the grated kohlrabi in a clean towel. Roll up the towel and squeeze it tightly to drain any excess water. This step is really important, otherwise the tzatziki will be too watery.
2. Mix the grated kohlrabi with the yogurt. Add the dill and mint. Add the garlic (depending on how garlicky you want it), lemon juice, and salt. Mix everything together with a spoon, then place the tzatziki in the refrigerator for at least 30 minutes or up to 2 days before serving. Serve with a small drizzle of olive oil on top and additional herbs (if you like) and a little salt and pepper.

NOTE: You can use either cow's milk or sheep's milk Greek yogurt. But in both cases, this recipe requires Greek yogurt because a classic yogurt does not have enough thickness to produce a sufficiently creamy tzatziki.

Tomato and Goat Cheese Dip

Serves: 4 to 6

Preparation time: 5 minutes

¾ cup (128 g) sun-dried
   tomatoes in oil
1 cup (237 g) artichokes in oil
¾ cup (170 g) goat cheese
½ teaspoon smoked
   paprika, optional
Sea salt to taste
XL Herbes de Provence
   (page 22) to taste
Buckwheat Chips (page 67) or
   other crackers or crusty bread
   for serving

After getting burned out on the overuse of sun-dried tomatoes in the '90s, I'm ready to eat them again! I think they are best when used judiciously, but I must say they can really do wonders to sauces in terms of flavor and texture, because when blended they add a lot of depth. This dip can also be made with cream cheese instead of goat cheese if you're in a serious pinch.

1. Drain the sun-dried tomatoes and artichokes, but don't rinse the oil. Add the sun-dried tomatoes and ¾ cup of the artichokes to the bowl of a food processor along with the goat cheese. Blend until smooth. Add the smoked paprika if you're using and taste for salt. I usually don't end up adding salt, as most marinated store-bought vegetables are high in salt already. But if you've made your own sun-dried tomatoes and artichokes in oil, you might want to add a little salt.
2. Spoon the dip into a shallow bowl. Chop the rest of the marinated artichokes and place on top of the dip along with a little XL herbes de Provence. Serve with the buckwheat chips.

Seasonal Tzatziki

Tomato and Goat Cheese Dip on Buckwheat Chips

Herbes de Provence–Fried Camembert (or Brie) with Pickled Red Onions

Serves: 2 to 4
Preparation time: 10 minutes
Cooking time: 2 to 3 minutes

Vegetable oil for deep-frying
1 tablespoon flour
½ teaspoon salt
2 teaspoons dried thyme
1 egg
8 ounces (227 g)
    Camembert or Brie
¼ cup (21 g) Herbed Bread
    Crumbs (page 27) or use
    store bought
2 tablespoons XL Herbes de
    Provence (page 22) or thyme
1 handful of mesclun greens
2 tablespoons Pickled Red
    Onions (page 203)
1 tablespoon Mustard Seed
    Caviar (page 34)

While somewhat kitsch, an occasional treat of fried cheese is undeniably indulgent and irresistible. I like to play on the herbiness of Normand-style cheese with lots of thyme. Serve this with some baguette slices or simply a few spoons.

1. Heat the vegetable oil over medium heat in a deep saucepan. The saucepan should be large enough that the oil only comes up halfway.
2. Stir together the flour, salt, and thyme. Beat the egg in a small or medium bowl.
3. Dredge the cheese (without cutting it) through the flour mixture. Dip and evenly coat the cheese in the egg and cover with the bread crumbs and XL herbes de Provence or thyme, pressing on the sides so that it sticks well.
4. Place the cheese in the saucepan with tongs or a skimmer and deep-fry for 2 to 3 minutes until golden. Remove it carefully and place on paper towels for 1 minute to absorb any excess oil.
5. Serve hot over mesclun greens with pickled red onions and mustard seed caviar on top.

Buckwheat Chips

Yield: 7 ounces (200 g)
Preparation time: 10 minutes
Cooking time: 15 minutes

1½ tablespoons olive oil
4 Buckwheat Galettes
  (page 204)
½ teaspoon salt
1 tablespoon Za'atar (page 26),
  completely optional

I make these chips at least once a week, and they grace my coffee table for most get-togethers, as they pair nicely with almost any type of dip. I'd suggest you try them as they are with sea salt or topped with Za'atar. Serve with the Tomato and Goat Cheese Dip (page 63), one of the olive tapenades (pages 55 or 58), or the Red Pepper Tartinade (page 61). For a completely different direction, sprinkle shredded Comté cheese on top, broil for 2 minutes, and call them (French-style) nachos!

1. Heat the oven to 350°F (180°C). Brush two baking sheets with the olive oil, using either a pastry brush or simply your fingers and a little paper towel. Cut the galettes into largish 3-inch-wide (8 cm) chips (strips, squares, or triangles—the shape is up to you). Divide the chips between the baking sheets. Turn the chips over so that the side up has olive oil on it and the bottom side cooks in the remaining oil. Sprinkle with the salt and Za'atar, if using. Bake until they are deep brown and crispy, about 15 minutes. Let cool and then store in an airtight container at room temperature for up to 2 weeks.

Flute Crackers with Cheese and Seeds

Serves: 2 to 4
Preparation time: 15 minutes
Cooking time: 14 minutes

8½ ounces (245 g) pâte feuilleté (see below) or store-bought puff pastry

2 eggs

2 tablespoons grated cheese (cheddar, Parmesan, Comté, Swiss, Gouda)

1 tablespoon plus 1 teaspoon poppy seeds

1 tablespoon plus 1 teaspoon sesame seeds

Sea salt

When I divorced, I didn't entertain much at first. I had a new apartment to set up while being a mom and paying bills on my own. But when I finally did start having friends over, I realized that the way I wanted to entertain had changed. I didn't want to be in the kitchen alone with my glass of wine; I wanted the kitchen to be where I cooked but also where I socialized. So I built a simple bar that overlooks my kitchen counter (and also doubles as extra counter space when need be). My tastes changed too. I liked lighter, more vibrant red wines. And I liked lots of small plates, easy to share and socialize around. These lovely crackers are perfect for doing just that.

For such little effort, these crackers are far, far better than any store-bought version. As a bonus, when I'm busy preparing something else I can even get my kids to make these because they are honestly really enjoyable to sprinkle and twist up. The variations are quite endless: stone-ground mustard and cheese, Walnut Jam (page 44), Green or Black Olive Tapenade (pages 55 and 58, respectively), and spreadable goat cheese with Ramp Leaf Oil (page 36). I often double the amount of crackers and choose a different variation for my second batch.

1. Preheat the oven to 350°F (180°C). Roll out the pâte feuilleté into a square (10 by 10 inches; 25 by 25 cm). Separate the egg yolks from the whites and reserve the egg whites. Beat the egg yolks and then spread this across the feuilleté with a pastry brush. Sprinkle the cheese and a tablespoon each of the poppy seeds and sesame seeds on top. Sprinkle with a little sea salt.

2. Cut the pâte feuilleté into eight rectangles of the same size. Lift up a section, twist each end in opposite directions, and place on a lightly oiled or parchment-lined baking sheet. Repeat with the rest. Beat the egg whites until slightly foamy and brush it over the twists. Sprinkle with the remaining poppy seeds, sesame seeds, and a pinch of sea salt. Bake for 12 to 14 minutes, until deep golden and puffy. Store the twists in an airtight bag or box for up to 1 week.

Pâte Feuilletée

Makes: 8½ ounces (245 g)
Preparation time: 10 to
15 minutes
Rest time: 45 minutes

8½ ounces (240 g) cold butter
1¼ cup (200 g) white flour
4 teaspoons sugar
⅔ teaspoon salt
6 tablespoons (89 ml) water

1. Cut the butter into small ½-inch pieces. Add the flour, butter, sugar, and salt to the bowl of a stand mixer. Mix together with a paddle attachment for 2 to 3 minutes or by hand for 5 to 6 minutes until the mixture is fairly homogenous. Add the water and mix again until smooth, but not too smooth—small bits of butter should still be visible. Remove the dough from the bowl, form it into a ball, and wrap it tightly with plastic wrap. Refrigerate for 45 minutes.

2. Place the dough on a lightly floured surface. Roll out the dough into a long rectangle, approximately 24 by 7 inches. Fold one-third of the pastry on top of the center and then the other third, so that there are now three layers of dough. Flatten the dough with a rolling pin to form another rectangle the same size as the first. Repeat the same folding techniques again and flatten again. Roll out the dough a third time and fold into another rectangle. Your pâte feuilletée is now ready to be used or can be stored in the refrigerator, tightly wrapped for up to 3 days prior to using.

Radish Toasts with Pistou Butter

Serves: 4
Preparation time: 10 minutes
Rest time: 45 minutes
Cooking time: 3 minutes

2 tablespoons Le Pistou
  (page 34)
2 tablespoons softened (but not
  melted) butter
10 to 15 small radishes,
  thickly sliced
4 to 6 large slices of
  country-style bread
Pickled Red Onions
  (page 203), optional
Za'atar (page 26), optional
Sea salt

These toasts not only come together quickly, but for me, they also hit the mark for an indulgent yet balanced predinner snack. I most often use breakfast radishes for their mild flavor and crowd appeal. To give this recipe year-round possibilities, you can substitute more pungent varieties such as black radish or vibrant red meat radish. If the radishes that I use have their greens attached, I usually mince up a tablespoon or so and add it to the pistou butter for a little extra texture. You can even make your Le Pistou (page 34) with half basil leaves and half radish leaves.

1. Incorporate the pistou with the butter using a whisk or the back of a fork. Place the butter in the refrigerator for at least 45 minutes to let it firm up.
2. Wash and dry the radishes. Toast the bread and cut it into approximately 3-inch (8 cm) squares or rectangles. Allow the toast to cool and then spread with the pistou butter. Place the radish slices on top of each toast, add a few pickled red onions and a pinch of za'atar, if using, and sea salt. Serve immediately, or place in the refrigerator for up to 30 minutes just before serving.

Tempura-Fried Squash Blossoms

Makes: 16 to 20
squash blossoms
Preparation time: 20 minutes
Cooking time: 12 minutes

16 to 20 squash blossoms
   (see Note)
4 cups (792 ml) vegetable oil
½ cup (60 g) flour or rice flour
1 teaspoon salt
1 egg yolk
⅔ cup (151 ml) water
Fresh herbs for topping
Lemon-Herb Yogurt Remoulade
   (page 44) for serving

Squash blossoms are some of summer's simplest, and cheapest, pleasures—especially if you grow them yourself. Many an easy weeknight dinner starts with a handful of squash blossoms that I pluck from my boyfriend's garden. Though the most commonly used squash blossom comes from zucchini, all squash blossoms are edible, so you don't have to limit yourself to a particular squash.

Blossoms are best picked when they are fully open. You can then store them in the fridge for up to 3 days before use. I often collect the blossoms over the course of a couple days in order to have a good amount on the table, but you can cut the recipe in half if you have less.

1. Clean the squash blossoms: Rinse them in cold water, remove the pistil, and pat dry with paper towels. Trim the stems to the base of the blossom.
2. In a deep saucepan, heat the vegetable oil to 350°F (180°C). Line a plate with paper towels and set it off to the side.
3. Whisk together the flour and salt in a medium bowl. Add the egg yolk and water and whisk again until the batter is smooth. Dip the squash blossoms one by one into the batter. Run your fingers over the blossom to remove excess batter, they should just be lightly coated (too much batter makes for doughy blossoms). Set the blossoms on another tray or plate as you go along. Working in 3 or 4 batches, fry the blossoms for 2 minutes, or until uniformly golden, turning each blossom with tongs or a fork halfway through cooking. Remove from the oil and set on your paper towel–lined plate.
4. Serve the squash blossoms on a large plate sprinkled with fresh herbs. Serve with the lemon-herb yogurt remoulade on the side.

Tempura-Fried Sage Leaves

Serves: 2 to 4
Preparation time: 5 minutes
Cooking time: 5 to 6 minutes

FOR THE TEMPURA

1 teaspoon salt
½ cup (60 g) plus 2 tablespoons
   flour
1 egg yolk
⅔ cup (151 ml) water
4 cups (792 ml) vegetable oil for
   frying (safflower, canola)
6 sage sprigs

FOR THE HARISSA AIOLI

¼ cup (57 g) Mayonnaise
   (page 40)
½ teaspoon minced garlic
½ teaspoon salt
½ to 1 teaspoon Red Pepper
   Harissa (page 39) or
   Espelette pepper or other hot
   sauce or chili powder

Once I got the hang of tempura—not that it's all that difficult—I started frying all sorts of thinly sliced vegetables as well as hearty greens, such as kale and carrot tops. I got the idea to fry sage leaves from Deviant, a natural wine bar in Paris' 10th arrondissement. In the South of France, most people have sage growing in their garden. It grows pretty rampant and this little tempura trick seemed pretty ideal for making the most of it.

1. Prepare the tempura batter: Stir together the salt and flour. Add the egg yolk and water. Whisk until combined but take care not to overmix.
2. Make the harissa aioli: Stir together the mayonnaise, garlic, salt, and harissa. Set aside.
3. In a deep saucepan or deep fryer, heat the oil to 350°C (180°C). Do not overfill the pan or fryer. If frying in a saucepan, make sure the oil does not exceed half of the pan.
4. Prepare a plate covered with paper towels (or a kitchen towel). Dip a sage sprig into the tempura batter with tongs or chopsticks. Place it in the hot oil. Fry for 1 to 2 minutes, flipping midway once it is slightly browned. Use tongs, chopsticks, or a skimmer to remove the sage sprig from the oil and place on the paper towel–lined plate. Repeat with the remaining sage sprigs. If frying more than one sprig at a time, make sure they don't stick to each other. Serve the sage leaves directly on the stems with the aioli for dipping on the side.

Pissaladière with Onions and Olives

Serves: 4 to 6
Preparation time: 20 minutes
Cooking time: 1 hour
25 minutes

2 tablespoons olive oil
1½ pounds (680g) yellow or
   white onions, peeled and
   thinly sliced
½ teaspoon minced garlic
⅓ cup (78 ml) white wine
1 teaspoon sugar
1 teaspoon thyme
½ teaspoon salt
8 ounces (225 g) puff pastry or
   Pâte Feuilleté (page 71)
10 olives
1 tablespoon capers
1 to 2 tablespoons XL Herbes
   de Provence (page 22)

This recipe always reminds me of an awkward date I had just after I first moved to France. We were both short on cash and couldn't speak each other's language (he was Italian and neither of us spoke decent French), but we spoke food together. So we decided to make dinner. When I arrived at his place, the kitchen was pungent with onions. We would be preparing an onion sauce to serve over pasta. You could say we got to know each other as we cried while peeling the 10 onions needed for the recipe. I was dubious and figured that kissing would be off the table after this meal, but once the onions were simmered down, they turned into a surprisingly mild confit. Like that pasta, this tarte (which comes from the city of Nice, on the Italian border) always reminds me of what you can do with just a few simple ingredients. If you are running short on either olives or capers, just add a little extra of whichever you have so as not to miss out on the salty brininess for which pissaladière is known.

1. Heat the olive oil in a large frying pan over medium-low heat. Add the onions, garlic, white wine, sugar, thyme, and salt. Gently cook for 30 to 40 minutes, until the onions are translucent and have reduced in volume by half. Lower the heat a little if the onions begin to brown.

2. Preheat the oven to 350°F (180°C) and lightly oil a baking sheet. Roll out the puff pastry into approximately a 12-by-10-inch (30-by-25 cm) rectangle. Place it on the baking sheet. Make a rough crust by folding in the sides and corners, pressing them down with the back of a fork. They don't need to be perfect. Spread the onions over the center of the pastry, allowing them to slightly spill over onto the crust. Place the olives on top along with the capers and Herbes de Provence. Bake for 40 to 45 minutes, until the crust is golden brown. Allow the pissaladière to cool. Cut to serve.

Oeufs Mayonnaise with Fried Capers

Serves: 4
Preparation time: 15 minutes
Cooking time: 14 minutes

6 medium eggs, organic
(see Note)
2 tablespoons capers
2 tablespoons olive oil
1 tablespoon fresh rosemary
Sea salt
¾ cup (170 g) Mayonnaise
(page 40)
Espelette pepper or chili
powder, optional
Mustard Seed Caviar
(page 34), optional

This dish is more or less the cousin of deviled eggs. The difference is that the yolks are left intact, and rather than stuffing the eggs, you cover them with mayonnaise. Some bistros, like Le Comptoir du Relais on the left bank, cover the eggs with so much mayonnaise that the egg is no longer visible. Whether you spoon the mayonnaise with a heavy hand or not, you'll want to serve these with a little bread for mopping up any leftover mayonnaise or bits of fried capers. And go ahead and change up the topping. My rule is to always add something briny on top—capers, pickles, olives, Mustard Seed Caviar (page 34)—as well as something crunchy—fried herbs, crispy shallots, Toasted Buckwheat (page 29), Herbed Bread Crumbs (page 27). Make these what you want!

1. Bring a medium pot of water to a boil and prepare a cold water bath. Place the eggs gently in the pot with a skimming spoon or other large spoon. Boil for 7 to 9 minutes, depending on how cooked you like your yolks. I like mine cooked at 7 minutes 30 seconds, resulting in an egg that's jammy on the inside with the whites more or less firm and therefore not too difficult to peel. For a firmer yolk (and white), add on another minute or two. When the eggs are done cooking, immediately place them in the cold water bath for 3 minutes, then allow them to cool in their shells at room temperature. Hot eggs are more fragile than cold, so wait to peel them when they have cooled down, at least 20 minutes.

2. In the meantime, make the fried capers. Gently press the capers between the folds of a kitchen towel in order to remove as much liquid as possible. Heat half the olive oil in a small frying pan over medium heat. Add the capers and pan fry them for 1 to 2 minutes, until the edges are crispy and golden. Remove them and place on a paper towel. Heat the rest of the oil and fry the rosemary for 2 to 3 minutes, until the edges are crispy and golden. Lightly salt the rosemary, remove from the pan, and place on a paper towel.

3. Peel the eggs and slice them in half lengthwise. Place them on a serving plate. I like to place half the eggs with the flat side down, this keeps them from slipping around on the plate. Spoon the mayonnaise on top of each egg and sprinkle with the fried capers, rosemary, and sea salt. I also like to top them with a little Espelette pepper and mustard seed caviar. Serve immediately or keep in the refrigerator for up to 2 hours before serving.

NOTE: The cooking time for your eggs can vary depending on their size and temperature. A small egg will cook 1 minute faster than a medium egg, and a large egg will take 1 to 2 minutes more. A cold egg will take 30 seconds longer to cook compared to a room temperature egg, so keep this in mind. If you are cooking more than 6 eggs, I would suggest boiling the eggs in batches, as overcrowding the pot can also change the cooking time.

Pissaladière with Onions and Olives

Oeufs Mayonnaise with Fried Capers

Butternut Beignets with Spicy Aioli

Serves: 4 to 6
Preparation time: 15 minutes
Cooking time: 15 to 20 minutes

¾ pound (340 g)
  butternut squash

1 cup (120 g) flour

1 teaspoon baking powder

2 eggs

¾ cup (75 g) grated cheese
  (Parmesan, Cheddar,
  mozzarella, Comté, Gouda)

¼ cup minced scallions

½ teaspoon minced garlic

1 teaspoon smoked paprika

1 teaspoon Espelette pepper
  or equivalent

1 teaspoon salt, more to taste

4 cups (792 ml) vegetable
  oil for frying (canola,
  sunflower, peanut)

⅔ cup (75 g) Aioli (page 40)

2 teaspoons Red Pepper
  Harissa (page 39)

½ lemon, for juicing

This is one of my go-to recipes when I want to serve something impressive and equally indulgent at aperitif hour. There aren't many occasions for preparing fried food ahead of time, but this is certainly one of them. I usually prepare these up to a day ahead of time, and prior to serving pop them in the oven for 8 to 10 minutes at 350°F (180°C). They crisp up even more because they tend to lose a little oil in the reheating process. In the warmer months, I use zucchini in place of butternut squash. If you do the same, just make sure to thoroughly squeeze out the water from the zucchini after grating it.

1. Wash and dry the butternut squash. There is no need to peel it. Grate it with either a box grater or cut into large chunks and grate in a food processor on the largest grade so that it resembles shredded cheese. Wrap it in a towel and squeeze out any excess moisture. This will make for crispier beignets. Place the grated squash in a medium bowl. In a separate bowl stir together the flour and baking powder. Pour the flour mixture over the squash and stir well. Then add the eggs, grated cheese, scallions, garlic, paprika, Espellette pepper, and salt and stir well to combine.

2. Heat the vegetable oil to 335°F (170°C), in a deep saucepan or pot, making sure it doesn't fill the pot or pan more than halfway in order to deep-fry comfortably. If you don't have a thermometer, see Note below. Using a soup spoon, test your first beignet by gently placing one spoon of the batter in the hot oil. Use another spoon to scrape the batter off and into the oil. Turn it over once during cooking to ensure it browns evenly. When you think it is cooked through, cut it in half to verify. If it browns too fast, it won't be cooked on the inside. If this happens, turn down the heat and try again. Once the temperature is right, cook small batches of 5 or 6 beignets to fry safely and prevent overcrowding. Place the fried beignets on a paper towel–lined plate to absorb excess oil.

3. Stir together the aioli and red pepper harissa. Season to taste with salt. Squeeze the lemon over the beignets and serve with the spicy harissa aioli on the side for dipping.

NOTE: If you don't have a thermometer, test a beignet by placing it into the oil. It should float to the top and turn golden in 3 to 4 minutes. If it takes longer, turn the heat up; if it cooks too quickly, turn the heat down.

Smoky Cheese Gougères

Makes: 24 gougères
Preparation time: 10 minutes
Cooking time: 17 minutes

5 tablespoons butter, plus
  1 teaspoon for baking sheets

1 teaspoon table salt, plus
  more to taste

1 cup (227 ml) boiling water

1 cup (120 g) flour

4 eggs

1 cup (113 g) plus 1 tablespoon
  grated cheese

4 tablespoons scallions, minced

1 teaspoon smoked paprika

Freshly ground black pepper

⅔ teaspoon fleur de sel

Fairly effortless, yet impressive, this is one of those recipes that I come back to often when I'm looking for something slightly substantial to serve at apéro time. Gougères don't require fancy ingredients, and if you're missing one of the herbs or spices, don't hesitate to replace it with another. But if you are feeling especially fancy, then whip out a pastry bag (a trimmed zip-lock plastic bag will also do) and pack it with 5 tablespoons of either spreadable goat cheese or ricotta. You'll just want to season the filling first with some XL Herbes de Provence (page 22) and a pinch of smoked paprika. Using a longer or pointed piping tip, fill the warm gougères with a small amount of the seasoned cheese and serve immediately.

1. Preheat oven to 450°F (230°C) and lightly butter two baking sheets. Melt the 5 tablespoons of butter with the salt, then add the boiling water to a medium sized saucepan over low heat. Turn off the heat and quickly whisk in the flour. The dough should pull away from the sides of the saucepan. If it doesn't, then turn on the heat for another minute while whisking.

2. Add the eggs one at a time, mixing well between each addition. Stir in the grated cheese, scallions, smoked paprika, table salt to taste, and pepper.

3. Using a tablespoon, scoop out balls of dough and place them on the baking sheet about 2 inches (5 cm) apart. Sprinkle with the fleur de sel. Bake for 5 minutes, then lower the temperature to 410°F (210°C) and bake for 10 to 12 minutes more, until the gougères are golden brown. Allow them to cool on the baking sheet for 5 minutes before serving.

Panisse Chickpea Flour Frites

Makes: 12 frites
Preparation time: 10 minutes
Rest time: 12 hours
Cooking time: 14 minutes

5 tablespoons butter or olive oil
1⅓ cups (302 ml) water
⅓ cup (28 g) chickpea flour
½ teaspoon salt
½ teaspoon Espelette pepper
4 cups (792 g) neutral vegetable oil (canola, sunflower, safflower)
Sea salt to taste
Fresh thyme to serve
Freshly grated cheese to serve
4 tablespoons Aioli (page 40), Mayonnaise (page 40), Red Pepper Harissa (page 39), or a combination, optional

Typical street food in the South of France, and Nice in particular, these frites almost have a quality similar to cheese just after being fried. After a few minutes of frying, the chickpea batter becomes crispy on the outside and addictively gooey and stretchy inside, similar to mozzarella sticks. I've even fried them the night before and then reheated them the next day in the oven at 350°F (180°C) for 5 minutes with great results. You can enjoy these light fries with Red Pepper Harissa (page 39), Aioli (page 40), or with a combination of the two. And if you'd like them vegan, then go ahead and use olive oil in place of the butter.

1. Lightly oil a small baking sheet or oven pan. Bring 1 cup of the water and the butter to a boil in a medium saucepan. In a small bowl, whisk together the remaining ⅓ cup water and the chickpea flour, salt, and Espelette pepper. Use a spatula to quickly scrape this mixture into the pot of boiling water. Whisk the mixture energetically for 4 minutes over medium-low heat until the batter is smooth and it begins to thicken. Pour the mixture onto the baking sheet and form a 6-by-8 rectangle (15 by 20 cm) that is about 1 inch (3 cm) thick. Smooth the top of the mixture with the spatula— wet the spatula before smoothing to keep it from sticking. Refrigerate for at least 12 hours and up to 2 days.

2. Cut the panisse into thick ¾-inch (2 cm) fries. Heat the vegetable oil to 350°F (180°C) in a deep saucepan or pot and line a plate with paper towels. If you don't have a thermometer, test a small piece of panisse by placing it into the oil. It should turn golden in 3 minutes. If it takes longer, turn up the heat; if it cooks too quickly, turn down the heat. Fry the panisse frites in small batches of 4 or 5 to keep them from sticking. Place them on the paper towel–lined plate when cooked. Lightly salt the frites to taste and serve with thyme, grated cheese, and aioli, if using.

BOHÈME COOKING

Focaccia with Zucchini, Goat Cheese, and Herbs

Serves: 4 to 6
Preparation time: 10 minutes
Cooking time: 28 minutes

1 medium-large (½ pound; 227 g) potato, peeled and quartered

¼ cup (41 g) instant polenta

2 tablespoons dry active yeast

3 cups (360 g) flour

½ cup (114 ml) milk

½ cup (120 ml) beer (a pale ale or light beer works well)

1½ teaspoons sea salt, plus more to taste

½ cup (100 ml) olive oil

1 medium zucchini

½ cup (57 g) crumbled goat cheese, or more if you like

1 tablespoon rosemary and/or thyme

2 to 3 tablespoons capers, optional

Focaccia is best served the same day, but whenever I have leftovers I make focaccia crackers or croutons. In fact, sometimes I even make focaccia just to make these crackers and croutons. To do this, cut the focaccia into 1-inch (3 cm) slices and dip each side in a little olive oil, sprinkle with sea salt, and bake for 10 minutes at 350°F (180°C). When the focaccia comes out of the oven, you can either let the slices cool as crackers or cut them into ¾-inch (2 cm) cubes to make croutons. Store in an airtight container for 2 to 3 days.

The influence of Italian food culture in French cooking is evident, especially in the South of France. One such influence can be seen in many boulangeries: freshly baked focaccia lined up next to the baguettes. This recipe is an adaptation from Simone Zanoni, an Italian chef who has been running the kitchen in one of the most undeniably French hotels, George V. It's the kind of recipe I make when I know I have time to let the dough rise but don't actually want to do very much active cooking. I simply throw whatever vegetables are in season on top along with a little cheese and herbs. Served alongside some greens and a simple vinaigrette, it's usually impressive enough in itself that I don't need to do much more than that.

1. Bring a medium pot of water to a boil and add the potatoes. Boil the potatoes for at least 8 to 10 minutes, until they break easily when pierced with a fork. Drain and mash the potato cubes. Measure out a cup of the mash and place in the bowl of a stand mixer (see Note). Add the polenta, yeast, flour, milk, beer, salt, and half of the olive oil. Using the hook attachment, knead the dough on low speed for 5 minutes and then on medium speed for 15 minutes. Remove the dough and place in a large, lightly oiled salad bowl. Cover tightly with plastic wrap and let the dough proof for about an hour, until it has practically doubled in size.

2. Remove the dough from the salad bowl and pull down the sides of the dough, forming a ball. There is no need to punch down the dough when making focaccia. Place the ball on a lightly floured surface. Add a little extra flour if the dough is too sticky, but only add the minimum. Roll out the dough with a rolling pin into a 12-by-10-inch (30-by-25 cm) rectangle and transfer to a lightly oiled baking dish. Using your fingers, poke holes all over the focaccia creating a crater-like surface. Drizzle the rest of the olive oil on top. Cover tightly with plastic wrap and let the dough rise for another hour.

3. Preheat the oven to 350°F (180°C). Using a vegetable peeler, cut the zucchini into long strips, about ⅛ inch (⅓ cm). Place the zucchini strips on top of the focaccia and sprinkle with the goat cheese, rosemary, capers, and sea salt. Bake the focaccia for 16 to 18 minutes until golden.

NOTE: I suggest you only make this recipe with a stand mixer or a food processor capable of handling dough. Yes, it's a little less bohème in regard to the material involved as compared to other recipes in the book, but focaccia dough is notoriously wet and kneading it by hand is just far too sticky an endeavor.

Salt-Roasted Celery Root "Charcuterie" with Fried Sage

Serves: 4 to 6
Preparation time: 15 minutes
Cooking time: 1 hour
Rest time: 1 hour

1 (1 to 1½ pounds; 454 to 680 g) celery root
3 tablespoons olive oil
1 pound (454 g) kosher salt
¾ cup (170 g) ricotta
2 tablespoons caper brine
Salt to taste
20 sage leaves
1 to 2 tablespoons capers
Bread to serve

Cooking entire root vegetables in a salt crust was a technique I learned from Alain Passard. He famously cooks his beets in a similar crust, repurposing a technique traditionally used for fish and applying it to vegetables. At his restaurant, before the salt crust is broken open, the dish is presented to much effect and pomp by white-gloved waiters, where the beets are then sliced tableside. The salt crust of this recipe not only imparts saltiness, but it also removes humidity, giving an unmistakable charcuterie flavor and texture to this humble vegetable.

1. Prepare the charcuterie: Heat the oven to 325°F (160°C). Wash and dry the celery root and peel the exterior layer. Rub with 1 tablespoon of the olive oil. Place half the salt in the center of a 15-inch (38 cm) square piece of aluminum foil. Lay the celery root on top and pull the aluminum foil around the sides of the celery, working the salt up the sides as well. Pour the rest of the salt on top of the celery root. Close the top of the foil as tightly as possible. Place in a small oven-safe pot and then place that in the oven for 1 hour.

2. Take out the celery root and let it cool before opening the aluminum foil, lest you give yourself a bad steam burn. Remove the salt crust from the celery root and rinse well. Let the celery root cool completely for about 1 hour. Cut it in half and then place in the freezer for 30 to 60 minutes, depending on how cold your freezer is set. You'll want to be very alert for the next part, so go ahead and pour yourself a glass of wine—but don't drink it just yet!

3. Prepare a mandoline slicer, or sharpen your best knife. If you happen to have a meat slicer (I know not many people do), you can take it out as it's amazingly efficient for slicing vegetables. Once the celery root has cooled and hardened, but is not completely frozen, remove it from the freezer. Using your mandoline or knife, slice it as thinly as possible, ideally around ⅛ to ¼ inch (⅓ to ½ cm) thick. If the celery root is too hard to slice, then let it rest at room temperature for 5 minutes and try again. Once you have finished slicing, lay your "charcuterie" on a flat plate.

4. Prepare the ricotta sauce: In a small bowl, whip together the ricotta and the caper brine. It's unlikely that you will need any salt, but taste the sauce just to make sure and salt to taste if necessary.

5. Wash the sage leaves and pat them dry. If they are not dry, they will spatter in the oil. Heat the remaining 2 tablespoons of olive oil in a saucepan over medium heat until it is hot, but not smoking. Place the sage leaves in the pan and cook on each side for approximately 30 seconds, or until the edges are slightly browned and crispy. Remove and set aside.

6. Serve the celery root charcuterie with the ricotta sauce and the capers and crispy sage leaves on top and some bread on the side.

NOTE: If you'd like to make this vegan, replace the ricotta sauce for a "creamy" vegan sabayon (see Asparagus with Creamy Vegan Sabayon, page 140).

Pickled Beet "Charcuterie" with Blue Cheese Sauce

Serves: 4 to 6
Preparation time: 10 minutes
Cooking time: 20 minutes

FOR THE PICKLED BEETS

½ cup (114 ml) white vinegar
1 cup (227 ml) water
1 tablespoon sugar
1 teaspoon salt
1 teaspoon coriander seeds
1 medium to large yellow or orange beet

FOR THE BLUE CHEESE SAUCE

2 tablespoons blue cheese or goat cheese
2 tablespoons yogurt or crème fraîche or sour cream
Salt to taste
Pepper to taste
1 tablespoon fresh tarragon or dill or chives
1 tablespoon Toasted Buckwheat (page 29)

This is a pretty glorious dish that comes together around one humble beet. I prefer lighter-colored beets such as yellow or orange for this, as red tends to color pretty much everything in its way.

Complementing the star of the dish is a bright, energetic sauce. Emulsifying the blue cheese with yogurt makes a little bit of a good cheese go a long way. Although this recipe could technically be a salad, don't hesitate to pile it all up—both beets and cheese yogurt—in between lightly toasted slices of sourdough, or tuck it all into a baguette with tarragon and even some extra herbs for a crunchy sandwich.

An extra little trick I've learned for dressing greens: The pickled beet juice from this recipe can be saved to make a lovely vinaigrette!

1. To make the pickled beets: Heat the vinegar, water, sugar, salt, and coriander seeds in a small pot over medium heat. Simmer for 5 minutes. Peel the beet (it will slice easier once peeled). Slice the beet thinly (⅛ to ¼ inch thick; ⅓ to ½ cm) with a mandoline or a sharp knife. Add the sliced beets to the poaching liquid and turn off the heat right away. Let the beets and the poaching liquid cool completely as the beets absorb all the flavor from the liquid, about 20 minutes. Remove the beets from the poaching liquid and simmer to reduce the liquid by half, about 15 minutes. Once the poaching liquid has reduced, reserve and set aside.

2. To make the cheese sauce: In a small bowl, mash the blue cheese with the back of a fork. Slowly incorporate the yogurt until you have a thick sauce-like texture. Season with salt and pepper to taste.

3. Serve the beets with the blue cheese sauce, tarragon, toasted buckwheat, and a couple spoonfuls of the pickling juice.

SMALL

(and Relatively Light)

PLATES

3

Although not necessarily a chapter only on salads, this section is where you will find them alongside various small dishes. Traditional French custom dictates that small salads be served alongside a meal or afterward as an accompaniment to a cheese course. But *salades composées* are the exception to the rule, generous and often composed of several vegetables and perhaps cheese or soft-boiled eggs. Oddly nonexistent on most restaurant menus, *salades composées* most often find their place in more casual cafés, bistros, and brasseries, especially those serving regional cuisine. The emblematic salad of Nice, *la salade niçoise,* has even received the protection of a French law, which aims to protect and promote the patrimony of certain recipes deemed culturally significant.

But don't worry, you should definitely feel free to interchange the vinaigrettes, or modify the greens in these salads. There are no laws here, and to this effect, I try to give examples as often as I can in regard to different options in the event you can't find a particular vegetable. Many possibilities abound—just take it lightly!

Endive, Apple, and Roquefort Salad

Serves: 4
Preparation time: 15 minutes
Cooking time: 7 minutes

½ cup (64 g) walnuts, chopped
1 green apple
1 tablespoon lemon juice
4 endives
2½ ounces (73 g) arugula,
 washed and dried
5 ounces (142 g) blue cheese
2 tablespoons Herbed Bread
 Crumbs (page 27), optional
½ cup (120 ml) Dijon Mustard
 Vinaigrette (page 42)

Endives make for a hearty and crunchy salad. They are often found year-round but grow especially well during the fall and winter months. This was one of the first traditional yet vegetarian salads that I discovered when I arrived in France. The French tend to favor simple green salads served with a meal or after the main course next to a cheese plate, but this is one of the vegetarian exceptions of the *salade composée.*

1. Preheat the oven to 350°F (180°C). Place the walnuts on a baking sheet and bake for 6 to 7 minutes, until slightly golden. Thinly slice the green apple and place it in a small bowl with the lemon juice and about 1 cup (227 g) water to keep it from discoloring.
2. Cut and discard about 1 inch (3 cm) of each endive stem. Thinly slice the endives lengthwise for a shredded effect, or slice it crosswise in circles if you prefer. To assemble the salad, either toss all the ingredients together or spread over a platter beginning with the endive, then the arugula, apple, blue cheese, walnuts, and bread crumbs. Drizzle the vinaigrette on top.

NOTE: To create a lovely variation on the Dijon Mustard Vinaigrette (page 42) for this salad, add a teaspoon of honey and blend a little walnut oil into the olive oil. Some crushed XL Herbes de Provence (page 22) wouldn't be out of place here either.

Veggie Niçoise Salade

Serves: 4
Preparation time: 15 minutes
Cooking time: 30 minutes

4 eggs
1 pound (454 g) small potatoes
1 tablespoon olive oil, plus more
   for serving
⅔ pound (300 g) zucchini
1 medium head of lettuce (bibb
   or romaine), washed and dried
2 medium tomatoes, cut
   in quarters
½ cup (71 g) olives
2 tablespoons capers
Sea salt
½ cup (120 ml) Dijon Mustard
   Vinaigrette (page 42)

When my friends and I gather in the summertime, we are often at least 12 adults at the table and plenty of kids. It can be hard to find a dish that pleases the whole table, but this salad pretty much has something for everyone. The fact that it's not mixed together but rather presented as a *salade composée* (with a light vinaigrette on the side) means that you can take what you like and leave what you don't. While there are always the traditional eggs, tomatoes, potatoes, greens, and olives in my *salade niçoise,* I leave the ingredients open-ended after that and add whatever looks best at the market. Depending on the time of year, this might be cucumber or green beans, but I also like to add any kind of vegetable that can be prepped and grilled ahead of time, such as zucchini and eggplant.

1. Bring a medium pot of water to a boil and prepare a cold water bath. Place the eggs gently in the pot with a skimming spoon or other large spoon. Boil for 7 to 9 minutes, depending on how cooked you like your yolks. I like mine cooked at 7 minutes 30 seconds, resulting in an egg that's jammy on the inside with the whites more or less firm and therefore not too difficult to peel. For a firmer yolk (and white), add on another minute or two. When the eggs have finished cooking, place them immediately in a cold water bath for 3 minutes. Then allow them to cool in their shells at room temperature. Hot eggs are more fragile than cold, so wait to peel them until they have cooled down, at least 20 minutes, and set aside.

2. Bring a medium pot of water to a boil. Peel the potatoes if you like, or leave the skin on. Cut the potatoes in half or in quarters, depending on their size so that they are not wider than 1 inch (3 cm). Boil them for 12 to 15 minutes, until tender. Rinse the potatoes with cold water and set aside.

3. Heat the olive oil in a large nonstick frying pan over medium heat. Cut each zucchini in half and then in ½-inch (1 cm) slices. Grill each side for approximately 3 minutes. Remove and set aside to cool.

4. To assemble, lay the lettuce leaves across a large serving plate. Cut the eggs in half and place them on the serving plate along with the potatoes, zucchini, tomatoes, olives, and capers. Drizzle with a little olive oil and sprinkle with sea salt. Serve with the vinaigrette on the side.

Apricot, Fennel, and Goat Cheese Salad

Serves: 2 to 4
Preparation time: 25 minutes
Cooking time: 5 minutes

FOR THE SALAD

1.8 ounces (51 g) goat cheese
   or feta or ricotta
1 cup sliced fennel
½ cup (114 ml) rice vinegar, or
   other white vinegar
1 cup (227 ml) water
1 teaspoon sugar
½ teaspoon salt
1 teaspoon fennel or anise
   seeds, optional
1 pound (454 g) apricots, halved
1 tablespoon fresh
   thyme, optional
2 tablespoons Toasted
   Buckwheat (page 29)
10 fresh basil leaves

FOR THE
HONEY VINAIGRETTE

2 tablespoons olive oil
2 tablespoons white wine or
   cider vinegar
1 tablespoon honey
1 tablespoon shallots, minced
½ teaspoon salt

Early in the summer, when apricots are still slightly firm, I like to feature them in a salad with bolder flavors such as goat cheese, basil, and marinated fennel. What's more, I like to add the goat cheese in an unconventional way: grating it over the apricots. To do this, I freeze the cheese first. This creates a "snow" of goat cheese with a lightness that doesn't overpower the apricots or other ingredients in the dish. This technique, which comes from a former sous-chef of the Café de la Paix in Paris, also works well with other cheeses that would normally be too soft to grate, such as blue or feta.

1. Place the goat cheese in the freezer for 45 minutes or up to the night before.
2. Prepare the pickled fennel: Heat the rice vinegar with the water in a small saucepan with the sugar, salt, and fennel seeds, if using. Simmer for 5 minutes and then turn off the heat. Add the sliced fennel to the brine and let it marinate until cooled, about 20 minutes. Drain before adding to the salad.
3. Prepare the vinaigrette: Whisk together all the vinaigrette ingredients.
4. To assemble, place the apricots on a serving dish, inside up. Spread the marinated fennel over the apricots and pour the vinaigrette over them. Sprinkle with a little thyme and toasted buckwheat. Add the basil leaves and, finally, grate the frozen goat cheese on top.

NOTE: I like to use fennel fronds to dress up the plate. They have a delicate, concentrated fennel flavor, and they are beautiful too.

Parisian Mushroom Salad

Serves: 4
Preparation time: 15 minutes
Cooking time: 20 minutes

FOR THE ONION CONFIT

2 tablespoons olive oil

1 large white onion, peeled and thinly sliced

4 tablespoons white wine

½ teaspoon minced garlic

½ teaspoon salt

FOR THE SALAD

1 medium black radish, thinly sliced

3½ ounces (99 g) aged cheese (Comté, Cheddar, Gouda), thinly sliced

6 medium button mushrooms, thinly sliced

½ cup (120 ml) Dijon Mustard Vinaigrette (page 42)

2 tablespoons Toasted Buckwheat (page 29)

A handful of Croutons (page 27), optional

Bread and cheese is a way of life in France. But when I overdo it on fondue or tartiflette, or too much wine, I turn to winter salads like this one for a hearty but slightly lighter meal. If you think that one can't eat delicious salads in the winter months then think again. Just toss together thinly sliced black radish and aged cheese with hearty mushrooms, Toasted Buckwheat (page 29), Dijon Mustard Vinaigrette (page 42), and a spoonful of onion confit.

1. Prepare the onion confit: Heat the olive oil over medium-low heat in a nonstick pan. Add the onion, half the white wine, garlic, and salt and simmer for 5 minutes until the wine is absorbed. Add the rest of the white wine, reduce the heat, cover, and cook for another 15 minutes. Remove the onion confit from the pan and let it come to room temperature.

2. Prepare the salad: Place the radishes in a medium salad bowl or plate and top with the sliced cheese and button mushrooms. Gently stir in the mustard vinaigrette and onion confit. Toss on the toasted buckwheat, a few croutons (or not), and serve right away.

Kale-Lentil Salad with Feta and Lemon-Thyme Vinaigrette

Serves: 2 to 4
Preparation time: 20 minutes
Cooking time: 15 minutes

FOR THE LENTILS
1 cup (198 g) green lentils
2 tablespoons olive oil
1 teaspoon thyme, fresh or dried
1 teaspoon coriander powder
½ teaspoon sea salt

FOR THE VINAIGRETTE
½ cup (112 ml) lemon juice
¼ cup (50 ml) olive oil
2 tablespoons vegetable oil
1 tablespoon crushed
  XL Herbes de Provence
  (page 22)
1 teaspoon Dijon mustard
1 teaspoon fresh or dried thyme
1 teaspoon sugar
½ teaspoon sea salt

FOR THE SALAD
5 ounces (145 g) kale, washed
  and dried, chopped
4 ounces (114 g) plus 2 tablespoons crumbled feta or goat
  cheese, for serving
¾ cup (133 g) cooked grains
  (quinoa, bulgur, farro)
½ cup (77 g) daikon or black
  radish, julienned
2 tablespoons red onion, minced
2 tablespoons Za'atar (page 26)
8 mint leaves, minced
½ lemon, sliced
4 eggs poached (page 212) or
  soft-boiled, optional

This combination of kale, lentils, and lemony vinaigrette makes for a vibrant and balanced winter salad. I first made this salad at a restaurant I consulted for on the Left Bank called Coffee Club. While it wasn't known for its vegetarian menu when it opened, after a few years the clients started coming specifically for veggie-focused salads like this one.

Add poached eggs or soft-boiled eggs on top if you're looking for something even more filling. And don't skimp on seasoning the lentils. Lentils are very absorbent and even better when dressed in olive oil and herbs, and then dressed again in a bright vinaigrette.

1. To make the lentils, bring a few quarts of water to boil in a medium pot. Pour in the lentils and cook, until tender but not falling apart, about 15 minutes. Drain the lentils and rinse with cold water to keep them from overcooking. Add the rest of the ingredients for the lentils and place in the refrigerator. This step can be done up to 2 days in advance.

2. To make the vinaigrette, place all the ingredients in the vinaigrette list in a blender and emulsify for 30 seconds.

3. In a medium-large salad bowl, stir together the lentils, kale, half of the feta, the grains, radish, red onion, and 1 tablespoon of the Za'atar. Pour in the vinaigrette and stir until the ingredients are thoroughly coated. Top with the rest of the feta, Za'atar, and the mint leaves. Serve with the sliced lemons and eggs if you are using them.

Tomato Carpaccio with Crispy Chickpeas, Stracciatella, and Fried Rosemary

Serves: 4
Preparation time: 15 minutes
Cooking time: 24 minutes

FOR THE CRISPY CHICKPEAS
1 cup (152 g) cooked chickpeas
1 teaspoon lemon zest
½ teaspoon sea salt
½ teaspoon Espelette pepper
½ teaspoon minced garlic

**FOR THE SUN-DRIED
TOMATO VINAIGRETTE**
¼ cup (43 g)
    sun-dried tomatoes
⅓ cup (67 ml) olive oil
⅓ cup (76 ml) vinegar (red wine,
    cider, champagne)
⅓ cup (76 ml) caper brine
2 tablespoons minced shallots
Sea salt to taste

FOR THE FRIED ROSEMARY
2 tablespoons olive oil
2 fresh rosemary sprigs

FOR THE SALAD
1½ pounds (680 g)
    tomatoes, sliced
8 ounces (226 g) Stracciatella
    or burrata
2 to 3 tablespoons capers

This recipe uses the best tomatoes of the summer along with fresh rosemary. I love to panfry fresh rosemary: It makes for a crispy topping, and because the flavor loses a little of its strength, you can use this slightly addictive topping with a heavier hand than uncooked rosemary. The rest of the ingredients are pantry staples like capers, chickpeas, and sun-dried tomatoes—for this last one, jarred are totally fine, but if you want to make a similar version of your own, use the recipe for Tomato Confit (page 30).

1. To make the crispy chickpeas, preheat the oven to 400°F (200°C) and prepare a baking sheet lined with parchment paper or lightly oiled. Toss the chickpeas with the lemon zest, salt, Espelette pepper, and garlic. Spread them on your baking sheet and cook in the oven until brown and crispy, 18 to 20 minutes, stirring once about halfway through. Remove the chickpeas from the oven and set aside to cool.

2. To make the sun-dried tomato vinaigrette, blend together in either a mortar and pestle or a blender the sun-dried tomatoes, olive oil, vinegar, caper brine, and shallots. Salt to taste, but keep in mind you may not need added salt if the caper brine is quite salty. Set the vinaigrette aside.

3. To make the fried rosemary, heat the olive oil in a small nonstick pan over medium-low heat and prepare a paper towel–lined plate. Fry the rosemary leaves until they become crispy but not brown, 3 to 4 minutes. Remove the rosemary from the pan and place on the prepared plate to absorb any excess oil. Once cooled, remove from the stems.

4. To assemble the salad, spread the tomatoes across a serving plate. Drizzle half the vinaigrette on top. Spoon the Stracciatella over the tomatoes. Sprinkle with the crispy chickpeas, fried rosemary, and capers. The dressing and toppings for this salad can all be made up to 3 days ahead of time, just keep them in airtight containers until use. Serve the rest of the vinaigrette on the side.

NOTE: I often use the juice from capers, or even olives, in place of or in addition to vinegar when making vinaigrettes. This double-duty trick is especially useful when I'm on vacation and don't want to do a lot of food shopping. The bright and briny flavor complements most fresh vegetables, and it gets the most out of what can be a slightly expensive condiment by using every last drop.

Fresh Cheese Dip with Fava Beans, Peas, and Mint

Serves: 4
Preparation time: 10 minutes
Cooking time: 1 minute

FOR THE CHEESE DIP
8 ounces (227 g) ricotta
4 ounces (114 g) goat cheese
½ teaspoon salt
1 cup (196 g) peas, shelled
1 cup (256 g) fava beans
2 tablespoons fresh
   mint, minced
2 tablespoons assorted minced
   herbs (basil, chives, dill)
1 teaspoon Za'atar (page 26)
2 tablespoons olive oil
2 tablespoons lemon juice
Small handful of micro greens
   such as pea shoots, optional
Sea salt

FOR SERVING
Sliced baguette
Crackers
Vegetable crudités (carrot
   sticks, radishes)

I use ricotta to make the most of, or to stretch out, other cheeses (goat cheese, feta . . .) if I happen to be a little short. When the cheeses are whipped and then topped with fava beans and garden peas, it makes for a light and almost virtuous cheese-like dip. Serve this dip when you want to cook as little as possible but still want to eat more than just a salad. If you can't get fresh beans and peas, you can make do with high-quality frozen ones.

1. For the cheese dip: Stir together the ricotta and the goat cheese with the salt. Depending on your goat cheese, the dip may be a little chunky; this is okay, but feel free to smooth it out with the back of a fork if you like. Spread the dip over a plate or serving platter.
2. Bring a small pot of water to a boil and blanch the peas and fava beans in the water for 45 seconds. Remove the peas and beans from the water immediately and rinse under cold water. Remove the waxy casing from the fava beans. Place the peas, beans, mint, herbs, and Za'atar in a medium bowl. Pour in the olive oil and lemon juice and toss until well coated. Spoon the greens over the cheese dip. Sprinkle with sea salt and serve with sliced baguette, crackers, and/or vegetable crudités.

Haricots Verts and Herb Salad with Walnut-Ginger Vinaigrette

Serves: 2
Preparation time: 10 minutes
Cooking time: 3 minutes

FOR THE WALNUT-GINGER VINAIGRETTE

2 tablespoons walnut oil

1 spring onion, minced top to bottom

1 tablespoon olive oil

1 tablespoon soy sauce

1 tablespoon stone-ground mustard

1 tablespoon apple cider or red wine vinegar

1 teaspoon ginger minced

FOR THE HARICOTS VERTS

1 pound (454 g) haricots verts, trimmed

2 handfuls of fresh herbs (cilantro, dill, chives)

1 handful of mustard greens or mesclun

In the early summer, when haricots verts are plentiful, I make this recipe on repeat. *Haricots verts* isn't just a translation for "green beans." They're actually a French variety of green beans, and are what I consider to be the most delicious type of bean. They are tender yet crunchy without any of the tough, fiber-like texture that you sometimes find in larger green beans. This is because haricots verts are harvested early.

While they are often a little more expensive, they are great for recipes like this one that take hardly any time on the stove. Be careful not to overcook them—you don't want to lose that tenderness. A tried-and-true method is to plunge them into cold water right after they come off the heat. If you prefer to use thicker beans, that is totally fine too! Just give them an extra minute or two of cooking time to reduce the toughness.

1. To make the vinaigrette: In a small bowl or measuring cup, whisk together all the vinaigrette ingredients and set aside.
2. To make the haricots verts: Bring a large pot of water to a boil. Drop the haricots verts into the boiling water and cook for 2 to 3 minutes, until just slightly tender. To avoid overcooking, strain the haricots verts and immediately rinse with cold water, gently turning them as you rinse to cool them quicker.
3. Once the haricots verts have cooled, place them in a medium-large salad bowl and toss them with the vinaigrette. Trim the fresh herbs into 2-inch (5 cm) segments, removing any long stems. Carefully stir the fresh herbs and mustard greens into the haricots verts. Serve immediately.

Fresh Cheese Dip with Fava Beans, Peas, and Mint

Haricots Verts and Herb Salad with Walnut-Ginger Vinaigrette

Crispy Leeks with Hazelnuts and Fried Sage

Serves: 2 to 4
Preparation time: 10 minutes
Cooking time: 30 minutes

⅓ cup (36 g) hazelnuts
4 medium leeks, white part only
1 tablespoon plus
   ½ teaspoon olive oil
8 sage leaves
½ cup (120 ml) Dijon Mustard
   Vinaigrette (page 42)
Mustard Seed Caviar (page 34)
Sea salt

Leeks are pretty much available year-round in France. Most leek dishes are either steamed or boiled, and the leeks are then served cold. But I also like to serve leeks hot, with seared, crispy grilled edges that I get from finishing them in a heavy cast-iron pan. A nonstick frying pan would also work, as would a lightly oiled BBQ tray set over hot coals.

If you can't get sage leaves, substitute with parsley, oregano, or rosemary. Whenever I return to Paris after a long weekend in the countryside, I always make sure to bring back lots of fresh herbs from the garden of whomever I am visiting. Almost anywhere you go in the French countryside, there is a good chance that there will be a garden. I once brought back a particularly big haul, and I couldn't even get my bag closed. Within a few minutes the train took on an herby aroma. Luckily, no one seemed to really mind. At home in my apartment, my kitchen is open to my living area, so I'm careful about what I cook, as the scent is bound to linger. For this reason, I don't fry garlic very often. But fresh herbs? All the time.

1. Preheat the oven to 350°F (180°C). Spread the hazelnuts out on a baking sheet and roast for 7 minutes. Allow them to cool and then roughly chop and set aside.

2. Bring a large pot of water to a boil. Gently clean the leeks and cut them crosswise into 4-inch (10 cm) pieces. You should get a total of 8 to 12 pieces, depending on the length of your leeks. Leave the pieces intact. Boil the leeks until relatively soft, about 10 minutes. Remove them with a skimmer or a slotted spoon and let them cool.

3. Once the leeks have cooled, press them in your hand or with the back of another plate to remove as much water as possible. If they lose their form a little that's all right. Heat a cast-iron or nonstick pan over medium-high heat. Brush the pan very lightly with ½ teaspoon of the olive oil. Place the leeks in the pan and cook on one side until the edges are seared and crispy, about 5 minutes. Flip them over and cook for another 3 to 4 minutes. Remove the leeks from the pan and set them aside.

4. Add 1 tablespoon of olive oil to the pan and fry the sage leaves. No need to turn them, they will quickly crisp up in less than 2 minutes. Remove the sage leaves from the pan and set aside.

5. In a small saucepan over low heat, gently warm the mustard vinaigrette for 1 to 2 minutes. Serve the leeks hot with the mustard vinaigrette, toasted hazelnuts, fried sage, mustard seed caviar, and sea salt.

NOTE: If you have any extra fried herbs, they will keep in an airtight container at room temperature for up to a week.

Artichokes à la Barigoule

Serves: 4
Preparation time: 30 minutes
Cooking time: 25 minutes

5 small purple artichokes
1 lemon
3 cups (750 ml) water
1 cup (125 ml) dry white wine
½ teaspoon salt
1 tablespoon thyme
1 tablespoon rosemary
1 tablespoon oregano
1 clove garlic, sliced
2 carrots
5 spring onions
1 handful parsley, minced
Extra virgin olive oil for drizzling
Fleur de sel
Freshly ground black pepper

Preparing artichokes can seem a bit intimidating, but with this little trick, you won't hesitate to grab a bunch the next time you are at the market. The advantages of this recipe are twofold. First, I like to make an unconventional kind of barigoule by using more cooking liquid than necessary. This way, I'm guaranteed tender artichokes and I also get a really fragrant artichoke broth in the process—perfect for flavoring a Spring Provençal Risotto (page 184). And second, although artichokes can be notoriously difficult to cut and shape when raw, you can give them another go once cooked, when the supple leaves can be easily trimmed with a pair of decent kitchen scissors.

1. Trim the artichokes: Remove any tough outer leaves until you get to the yellowish interior leaves. Place the artichoke on its side on a cutting board and cut off the top inch of the leaves. Cut the lemon in half and immediately rub it along the cut leaves to prevent too much discoloration as the leaves can oxidize after being cut. Then, trim the stems to 1¼ inches (3 cm) and peel them with a vegetable peeler to discard any of the tough outer skin. Pull off any remaining rough leaves and trim the edges of the leaves with a pair of scissors. Cut the artichoke in half or in quarters.
2. Add the water and wine to a medium saucepan that will fit your artichokes. Squeeze the juice from the lemon into the water and then add the salt, herbs, and garlic. Add the artichokes to the water and bring to a low boil. Reduce the heat and simmer for 5 minutes.
3. While the artichokes cook, peel and slice the carrots, cut the spring onions in half, and add both to the pot. Simmer for another 15 minutes. Drain the cooking liquid and save it to use as a broth for another time. Plate the artichokes and sprinkle them with parsley, drizzle with olive oil, and serve warm or at room temperature with fleur de sel and freshly ground black pepper.

Roast Cauliflower with Green Olive Tapenade

Serves: 4
Preparation time: 5 minutes
Cooking time: 20 minutes

1 small cauliflower
  (1½ pounds; 680 g)
1 cup (172 g) Green Olive
  Tapenade (page 58)
¼ cup (25 g) grated Parmesan
  cheese, optional
1 teaspoon olive oil
¼ fresh lemon
1 handful of washed and
  dried greens (mesclun,
  spinach, arugula)

This dish is one that you might be tempted to eat straight off the baking sheet. But if it makes it to the plate, I suggest serving it as a side dish to share. You can even toss it with some pasta, olive oil, and extra lemon juice. The Parmesan cheese makes the edges of the cauliflower become extra crispy, plus it's delicious.

1. Preheat the oven to 400°F (200°C). Wash and dry the cauliflower. Break it apart into 2-inch (5 cm) pieces and cut any larger parts down to size. Mix the green olive tapenade and Parmesan cheese (if using) together. In a large bowl, toss the cauliflower with the tapenade and cheese mixture to coat. If necessary, use your hands to coat the hard to reach spots.
2. Brush a baking sheet with the olive oil. Place the coated cauliflower on the baking sheet and cook for 18 to 20 minutes, until the edges are crispy and golden. Squeeze the lemon juice over the cauliflower. Serve immediately or let the cauliflower cool off a little until just slightly warm and serve over a handful of greens.

Charred Spring Onions on Yogurt

Serves: 2 to 4 people
Preparation time: 10 minutes
Cooking time: 10 minutes

¾ cup (170 g) Greek yogurt
1 tablespoon plus
   2 teaspoons olive oil
½ teaspoon garlic powder
1 tablespoon lemon juice
½ teaspoon salt
1 tablespoon pine nuts
¼ cup (36 g)
   hazelnuts, chopped
1 bunch spring onions or
   baby leeks
1 tablespoon lemon zest
2 teaspoons Za'atar
   (page 26) or 1 teaspoon
   dried thyme plus 1 teaspoon
   sesame seeds
Herbed Bread Crumbs
   (page 27), optional
Fresh herbs of your choice
   or XL Herbes de Provence
   (page 22)
Fleur de sel or sea salt

When friends show up for what is intended to be just a glass of wine, but unexpectedly turns into more, this is pretty much my go-to recipe. It's a little more substantial than just a dip, doesn't take more than five minutes at the stove, and can be slathered on bread—all important qualities for last-minute hosting.

The quality of the Greek yogurt is important here, as is the texture, so I would suggest a heavier full-fat variety over low-fat versions. Spring onions are great here for their slight bite, but young broccoli also works, as does spinach. If using the latter, just reduce the cooking time by half. Crunchiness comes from a few additional minutes of toasting the nuts and from homemade bread crumbs. But in a pinch, a bag of store-bought toasted nuts will be just fine. Depending on the season, I toss on some fresh herbs from my windowsill, or a handful of dried, chunky XL Herbes de Provence (page 22), and voilà!

1. Stir together the yogurt, 1 tablespoon of the olive oil, garlic powder, lemon juice, and salt. Place in the refrigerator while preparing the rest. Lightly toast the pine nuts and hazelnuts in a dry nonstick pan over medium heat for 4 minutes, stirring twice. Set the nuts aside to cool.

2. Prepare the spring onions by removing any discolored leaves and trimming the ends. Slice any large stalks, onion bulbs, or bottom ends in half lengthwise for easier cooking. Heat a nonstick or cast-iron pan over medium-high heat. Brush the pan with 1 teaspoon of the olive oil and sear the onions for 2 to 3 minutes on one side until charred. Then turn over and sear for another 2 minutes. Remove the onions and let them cool on a plate for a few minutes.

3. In the meantime, divide the yogurt between two to four plates. Place the onions on top of the yogurt. Drizzle with the remaining 1 teaspoon olive oil and serve sprinkled with the pine nuts, hazelnuts, lemon zest, Za'atar, bread crumbs, herbs, and fleur de sel.

Green Asparagus and Lentils with Labneh, Almonds, and Green Herb Oil

Serves: 4
Preparation time: 15 minutes
Cooking time: 22 minutes

¼ cup (20 g) slivered almonds
½ cup (99 g) green lentils
1 tablespoon lemon juice
Sea salt to taste
1 pound (454 g) asparagus, trimmed and halved
1 cup (8 ounces; 227 g) Marinated Labneh Balls (page 48) or store-bought
1 tablespoon sesame seeds or gomasio
Ramp Leaf Oil or Green Herb Oil (page 36) to serve
Fresh herbs of your choice, or ramp flowers

Although labneh does not have its roots in France (it is said to have originated in the Mediterranean region of Lebanon, Israel, and Turkey), it has gained a fast following among the French, who are prolific consumers of yogurt, labneh's main and almost sole ingredient. You can easily make your own labneh (see Marinated Labneh Balls, page 48), it just takes a little patience. But if you're in a pinch, mix together equal parts cream cheese and full-fat Greek yogurt for a similar texture and flavor. And if asparagus season has passed, don't hesitate to substitute with poached haricots verts or roasted slices of autumn squash.

1. Preheat the oven to 350°F (180°C). Place the almond slivers on a baking sheet and toast for 6 minutes.
2. Prepare the lentils: Pour the lentils into a small pot and cover with 2 cups of water. Bring to a boil and then simmer for 12 to 14 minutes, until just tender but not falling apart. Drain and season with lemon juice and a pinch of salt. Set aside to cool.
3. Prepare the asparagus: If the asparagus stalks are thicker than ½ inch (1 cm), slice them in half lengthwise. Bring a pot of salted water to a boil and prepare an ice bath. Poach the asparagus for 2 minutes. Remove the asparagus and place immediately in the ice bath in order to keep the color from fading.
4. To serve: Divide the labneh among four plates or spread it across one large platter. Place the lentils and asparagus spears on top, sprinkle with the toasted almonds and sesame seeds. Drizzle the green herb oil on top. Throw on a few fresh herbs or ramp flowers if you've got any and serve immediately.

Charred Spring Onions on Yogurt

BOHÈME COOKING

Green Asparagus and Lentils with Labneh, Almonds, and Green Herb Oil

Green Herb Gazpacho

Serves: 2 to 4
Preparation time: 15 minutes
Cooking time: 8 minutes

FOR THE GAZPACHO

1¼ pounds (567 g) zucchini, cut
    into ½-inch (1 cm) slices
⅓ pound (150 g) cucumber,
    peeled and cubed
8 to 10 (227 g) ice cubes,
    more if needed
2 handfuls of fresh herbs,
    packed (dill, basil, chives,
    tarragon), stems removed
2 tablespoons capers
2 tablespoons lemon juice
2 tablespoons olive oil
Salt to taste
4 tablespoons Greek yogurt or
    sour cream

FOR THE HERB SALSA

1 handful or 1 cup (61 g) herbs
    (basil, tarragon, dill), chopped
2 tablespoons scallions, minced
1 tablespoon spring
    onion, minced
1 tablespoon capers, minced
2 tablespoons lemon juice
1 tablespoon olive oil
½ teaspoon salt

This green herb and zucchini gazpacho draws acidity from the lemon juice while taking on the bright flavors of capers and handfuls of fresh herbs such as dill, basil, and tarragon. Even better, it takes less than 15 minutes to prepare thanks to a quick chill and a handful of ice cubes. This gazpacho is good on its own, but for a little more texture, serve it with an herb salsa.

1. To make the gazpacho, bring a large pot of water to a boil and add the zucchini. Steam or boil them for 7 to 8 minutes. Rinse under cold water until chilled. Add the zucchini to a blender with the cucumber and ice cubes and blend until smooth. Add the herbs to the blender with the capers, lemon juice, and olive oil and blend again until smooth. Add salt to taste, though often with capers, I find you don't need to add extra salt. Stir in a few extra ice cubes if necessary.
2. To make the herb salsa, stir together the fresh herbs, scallions, spring onions, capers, lemon juice, olive oil, and salt.
3. Serve the gazpacho cold with a small spoonful of Greek yogurt and the herb salsa.

Baby Beets with Stracciatella, Pistachios, and Currants

Serves: 2 to 4 people
Preparation time: 15 minutes
Cooking time: 40 minutes

1 pound (454 g) small beets
½ cup (138 g) white miso paste
¾ cup (176 ml) red wine
3 tablespoons sugar or honey
1 tablespoon thyme
2 tablespoons pistachios, shelled and chopped
8 ounces (226 g) Stracciatella or fresh mozzarella
¼ cup (36 g) currants or pitted cherries
1 tablespoon Fennel Hazelnut Dukkah (page 25), optional

Roasting beets with red wine and miso makes them quite irresistible. The slightly sweet earthiness of the beets also goes well with red berries and creamy cheese. The association of beets and berries takes inspiration from Sven Chartier, a Parisian chef who got his chops under Alain Passard. While Chartier is not a vegetarian chef, vegetables and terroir hold considerable importance in his cooking. So much so that, a couple years after receiving a Michelin star in Paris for his restaurant Saturne, he closed the restaurant and moved his family to the Perche, the green, folkloric countryside just west of Paris. There, he spent two years preparing a permaculture garden before opening a small restaurant subsistent on his own vegetables. The restaurant, which he runs with his wife and brother, is so successful that they need to open only four days a week, giving them a life-work balance that was never possible in Paris.

1. Preheat the oven to 400°F (200°C). Scrub and dry the beets. Peel them or leave the skin on; it's up to you. Cut the beets in half and slice them into half-moons. Place them in a medium salad bowl. Add the white miso paste, red wine, sugar, and thyme. Stir together and then sauté over medium heat in a cast-iron pot (Dutch oven) or oven-safe frying pan for 5 minutes. Place the pot in the oven, covered, and cook for 30 minutes. Stir occasionally. Remove the beets from the oven and let them cool.
2. Place the pistachios on a baking sheet and dry roast for 5 minutes. Let them cool and then roughly chop.
3. To assemble, place the beets on a serving plate, spoon the Stracciatella on top, add the pistachios, currants, and dukkah, and serve.

NOTE: If you don't have a Dutch oven or frying pan that is oven safe, just transfer the beets to an oven-safe pan and cover with a lid or foil.

HEARTY VEGETABLES

(as a Side or Even a Main)

4

Dishes from the recipes in this chapter can be made in varying sizes, from petite to grand. Spread across several small plates or put on a large platter, these are stars that can carry the show, so don't hesitate to scale them up for the dinner table. Leftovers can always be tucked into a baguette for a sandwich on the go the next day. In France, this on-the-go meal style often elicits a surprised-sounding "bon appétit" if you've got a mouthful while walking down the sidewalk—and even more so if you take it to the metro. Because in France, your meal isn't supposed be digested standing up, which is why lunch times still remain generous in spite of globalization and video calls. And dinner happens around 8 PM, latish by some standards, because it's meant to be the moment when your day is really, actually done—and that means all of it.

Artichokes for Dipping

Serves: 4
Preparation time: 15 minutes
Cooking time: 45 minutes
Rest time: 10 minutes

4 artichokes (about ¾ pound
    each; 340 g)
2½ quarts (2.5 L) water
2 tablespoons salt
2 tablespoons thyme
2 tablespoons rosemary
2 tablespoons oregano
2 garlic cloves, cut into quarters
1 lemon, cut in quarters
Caper and Herb Dipping
    Sauce (page 54) or
    vinaigrette of choice
Toasted Buckwheat (page 29)
    for serving

As much as I adore marinated artichokes and grilled artichokes, I almost prefer the ritual of eating an artichoke leaf by leaf. One by one, you pull off the leaves, dip them into a thick vinaigrette-like sauce, and then nibble on the tender ends. If you are lucky, the leaves will be thick and will get even plumper as you come closer to the center. Once you arrive at the center of the artichoke, there is just some maneuvering as you remove a few dense fibers with a knife, and a little nudge. Then, I'd suggest you stop to admire your work before you slowly devour the rest, dunking the smooth heart into the remainder of the sauce. For this last step, fork and knife are completely optional. Artichokes are one of the rare, yet sensual French meals that you can eat with your fingers. Just make sure to have some good cloth napkins and enough time at hand. I would suggest one per person, because, like some of life's other intimacies, artichokes are hard to share.

I like to poach the artichokes with a lot of herbs. You can also steam them, but I find I can always fit more in the pot when I don't have the steam basket inside! Between steaming and poaching, I've seen very similar end results.

1. Cut the stems off the artichokes so that they sit upright. Rinse and remove the first layer of large and fibrous leaves. Usually, you'll have to take off around six leaves per artichoke. You can trim the tops, but it's not necessary. Pour the water into a large pot and add the salt, thyme, rosemary, oregano, garlic, and lemon. Bring all of this to a simmer.

2. Once the water is simmering, place the artichokes in the pot bottom side down. You can either cook the artichokes all together (if they fit all at once in the pot!) or you can cook them two at a time. The cooking liquid should suffice for two rounds and become even more fragrant in the process.

3. Place a lid on the pot and gently simmer for 40 minutes. Depending on the size of the artichokes some might take another 5 minutes. Check if the artichokes are cooked through by turning one upside down and sliding a knife into the bottom. If it goes in easily, they are done. Remove the artichokes from the cooking liquid and place them upside down to cool and drain, approximately 10 minutes.

4. Serve the artichokes with the caper and herb dipping sauce and toasted buckwheat.

NOTE: I like to strain and reserve the cooking liquid—often in the freezer. It makes an excellent broth for artichoke risotto or a spring vegetable velouté.

Roast Jerusalem Artichokes with Fondue-Style Cheese Sauce

Serves: 2 to 4
Preparation time: 10 minutes
Cooking time: 23 minutes

1 pound (454 g) Jerusalem
   Artichokes (sunchokes)
2 teaspoons olive oil
1½ teaspoons salt
2 tablespoons butter
2 teaspoons flour
¼ cup (57 ml) milk
¼ cup (60 ml) dry white wine
   (beer can also be used
   in a pinch)
¼ cup (28 g) shredded cheese
   (white Cheddar or Comté)
Freshly ground black
   pepper to taste
XL Herbes de Provence
   (page 22), optional

As delicious as fondue is, it's also a really big investment in time and money, not to mention diet! This recipe comes quickly and is for when you want something fondue-ish on a smaller scale. But don't let that stop you from getting out the fondue picks if you'd like! You can also serve this with other roast vegetables such as potatoes, carrots, celery root, and more.

1. Preheat the oven to 375°F (190°C). Clean and trim the sunchokes; they should be firm. Remove any tough or soft spots. I like to leave the skin on, as I think it gives nice texture, but you can remove it if you wish. Cut the sunchokes into ½-inch (1 cm) thick slices. Place them in a bowl and toss with the olive oil and ½ teaspoon of the salt. Spread out on a baking sheet and roast for 16 to 20 minutes, until golden brown.
2. Melt the butter in a saucepan. Whisk in the flour followed by the milk and the wine. Whisk quickly until the sauce is smooth, about 3 minutes. Remove from the heat and add the shredded cheese little by little, whisking in between each addition. Stir in the rest of the salt and a little fresh ground pepper. Serve with the Herbes de Provence or just as is with the roasted sunchokes.

Oven-Baked Stuffed Zucchini Blossoms

Serves: 2 to 4
Preparation time: 20 minutes
Cooking time: 22 minutes

8 ounces (227 g) ricotta
1 lemon, zested
2 tablespoons capers
2 tablespoons fresh rosemary,
   minced, or 2 teaspoons dried
2 tablespoons fresh sage,
   minced, or 2 teaspoons dried
½ cup (50 g) grated Parmesan
½ teaspoon salt
½ teaspoon minced garlic
8 zucchini blossoms (see Note)
1 egg
3 tablespoons polenta
3 tablespoons buckwheat
   kernels, optional
1 lemon, cut in wedges

These oven-baked zucchini blossoms might seem intimidating, but preparing them is actually easy! They come together in just 10 minutes: Just remove the inner pistil of each blossom and stuff with ricotta filling, sprinkle with crunchy bits like polenta, Parmesan, and buckwheat, and bake. Cooking them in the oven makes for a light summer dish without the hassle of deep-frying. If you don't have zucchini blossoms, you can also use other types of Cucurbitaceae flowers, including cucumbers, melons, and squash, so don't hesitate to make this all summer long and well into the early fall.

1. Preheat the oven to 350°F (180°C) and lightly oil a baking sheet. Stir together the ricotta, lemon zest, capers, rosemary, sage, and half of the grated Parmesan. Add the salt and garlic and stir together again. Wash and pat dry 8 zucchini flowers, removing their pistils from the inside. Fill each flower with two spoonfuls of the ricotta filling. Gently close the petals around the filling, but no need to be a perfectionist, as they aren't being fried so there's no risk of losing a little filling. Place the blossoms on your baking sheet. Whisk the egg and gently brush it over the flowers. Sprinkle with any leftover minced herbs, the rest of the grated Parmesan, polenta, and buckwheat kernels, if using. These extra toppings will give the blossoms a little crunch. Bake the blossoms until slightly golden, about 22 minutes. Serve warm with lemon wedges.

NOTE: You can use zucchini blossoms with or without the zucchini attached. I really like zucchini when paired with the flowers. If you do too, don't hesitate. If you don't have the zucchini attached, you can also slice up one medium zucchini and add it to the pan.

Belgian Endive au Gratin with Béchamel

Serves: 4
Preparation time: 20 minutes
Cooking time: 45 minutes

FOR THE ENDIVES
6 large Belgian endives
1 tablespoon olive oil
½ teaspoon sea salt
2 tablespoons thyme,
  fresh or dried

FOR THE CLASSIC BÉCHAMEL
2 tablespoons butter
2 tablespoons flour
2 cups (454 ml) whole milk
1 cup (113 g) grated cheese
  (white Cheddar, Gruyère,
  Comté, Parmesan)
1 teaspoon sea salt
Freshly ground pepper,
  black or white

After I arrived in Paris and had (more or less) found my footing in the kitchen of the French family for whom I was an au pair, I decided to start seeking out new recipes. Fall had passed and I couldn't very well make ratatouille all winter. I had never cooked an endive before, but I was drawn to this recipe from the North of France and Belgium. The dish balances indulgent béchamel sauce that's baked over bitter greens.

Olivia, the mother of the family (and someone who thoroughly intimidated me), gasped and then erupted into laughter when I put the baked endives on the table. Apparently, she had never imagined an American cooking endives in France. The humor was slightly lost on me. In the end I earned a little more kitchen credibility that evening for having followed and successfully executed a meal from a recipe written in French—dictionary in one hand and a torn-out recipe from the pages of *Elle* magazine in the other. Little could I have imagined that 15 years later I would be writing those recipes myself.

1. To make the endives: Heat the oven to 325°F (160°C). Rinse and dry the endives. Slice the endives in half lengthwise. Lightly brush the endives with the olive oil, sprinkle with the salt and the thyme. Cook for 20 minutes in the oven, turning over once.

2. To make the béchamel sauce: Melt the butter in a medium saucepan on medium-low heat. Add the flour and whisk until combined and clumpy. Slowly pour in the milk, whisking constantly. As the milk heats up, the sauce will begin to thicken. When this happens, turn off the heat and add the grated cheese little by little, whisking constantly. Stir in the salt and pepper.

3. Place the endives in an 8-by-10-inch (20-by-25 cm) baking dish. Pour the béchamel sauce on top and bake until the top is bubbly and golden, 20 to 25 minutes. Serve right away.

NOTE: To complete the meal, serve with a green salad and bread on the side.

Brussels Sprouts with Gouda and Walnuts

Serves: 2
Preparation time: 5 minutes
Cooking time: 4 minutes

1 tablespoon walnut oil

½ pound (227 g) Brussels
  sprouts, trimmed and halved

¼ cup (28 g) walnuts, chopped

2 tablespoons rice vinegar
  (apple cider vinegar or white
  wine vinegar also work here)

2 tablespoons beer or dry
  white wine

1 tablespoon lemon juice

½ teaspoon minced garlic

1 teaspoon
  stone-ground mustard

Pinch of salt

2 ounces (57 g) Gouda,
  preferably aged

A friend of mine from a northern French town close to the Belgian border introduced me to the glorious combination of aged Gouda and mustard. The tangy cheese and mustard duo livens up many a vegetable (like carrots and celery, to name a couple), but I particularly like it on Brussels sprouts, which seems fitting for this northern France–inspired recipe. A sprinkle of Herbed Bread Crumbs (page 27) wouldn't be out of place to give this dish a little extra oomph. And if by chance you have leftovers, chop them up and toss them in with pasta and, of course, a little more grated cheese.

1. Heat the walnut oil in a heavy-bottomed nonstick pan. Once the pan is quite hot, but not smoking, add the Brussels sprouts and chopped walnuts. Sauté them for 2 minutes, turning just once halfway. Add the rice vinegar, beer, lemon juice, garlic, mustard, and salt. Continue to sauté for another 2 minutes. Remove from the pan. Grate half the Gouda on top and stir in. Let the Brussels sprouts cool for a few minutes and then grate the rest of the Gouda on top. Serve warm or at room temperature.

BOHÈME COOKING

Cauliflower au Gratin
with Herbed Bread Crumbs

Serves: 4 to 6
Preparation time: 20 minutes
Cooking time: 38 minutes

1 medium cauliflower

2 cups (500 ml) milk

2 tablespoons thyme (dry
   or fresh) or XL Herbes de
   Provence (page 22)

1 small garlic clove, minced

4 tablespoons butter

¼ cup (30 g) flour

1⅓ cups (151 g) grated Comté
   or white Cheddar cheese

½ teaspoon ground
   nutmeg, optional

1½ teaspoons salt

¼ cup (21 g) Herbed
   Bread Crumbs (page 27)

For me, this is really a quintessential winter meal. It's even a kid-friendly dish. I was quite impressed when my kids—who were quite young at the time—professed a love for my mother-in-law's cauliflower au gratin. It was heavy with cheese and it perfumed the whole house. She was a self-declared *femme moderne* and took satisfaction in the fact that she did little in the kitchen, so whenever she would invite us for Sunday lunch, I knew she was making an effort. I had never thought to prepare cauliflower for my kids, and had never even made it myself. I had planned to ask for the recipe, but it turned out that her au gratin wasn't exactly homemade. . . . In the end it didn't matter that I didn't get the recipe, as it was already enough to inspire my own au gratin making.

1. Preheat the oven to 350°F (180°C).

2. Steam the cauliflower: Break apart the cauliflower florets into 2-inch (5 cm) pieces. Place a steamer basket in a medium pot with a fitted lid. Fill the bottom with boiling water until it barely touches the steam basket—as you want to be careful not to boil the cauliflower. Cover and steam for 5 minutes. Remove promptly to prevent overcooking.

3. Prepare the béchamel: Pour the milk into a saucepan with 1 tablespoon of the thyme and the garlic and bring to a low simmer for 8 minutes. Remove from the heat. If you like, you can blend the milk with an immersion blender to deepen the flavor, or leave it as is. Melt the butter in a medium saucepan over low heat. Sprinkle in the flour and whisk together with the butter until combined. Whisking constantly, pour in the hot milk and continue to whisk until the sauce is smooth, 2-3 minutes. Turn off the heat and add the cheese, little by little in small handfuls, whisking it in each time before adding more. Whisk in the ground nutmeg and the salt. Add the cauliflower to the saucepan and stir to coat it completely in the sauce. Pour the cauliflower into an 8-by-10-inch (20-by-25 cm) oven dish. Sprinkle with the rest of the cheese, the last tablespoon of herbs, and the bread crumbs. Bake for 20 to 25 minutes, until bubbly and golden. Let cool 5 minutes before serving.

Asparagus with Creamy Vegan Sabayon

Serves: 2 to 4
Preparation time: 10 minutes
Cooking time: 15 minutes

FOR THE ASPARAGUS

½ cup (64 g) nuts
   (walnuts, hazelnuts)
2 pounds (907 g) asparagus
2 tablespoons Herbed Bread
   Crumbs (page 27)
2 tablespoons fresh herbs (dill,
   chives, basil)

FOR THE VEGAN SABAYON

½ cup (114 ml)
   unsweetened soy milk
2 tablespoons cider vinegar
1 teaspoon Dijon mustard
½ teaspoon minced garlic
1 teaspoon miso
   powder, optional
½ teaspoon salt, plus
   more to taste
1 cup (198 ml) vegetable oil
   (sunflower or grapeseed)
1 to 2 tablespoons lemon juice

Quickly steamed asparagus is one of spring's finest pleasures. In France, asparagus is often served cold, or warm, but rarely hot. This is probably due to the fact that it's usually steamed then placed in a cold-water bath to stop it from overcooking. You can use white or green asparagus for this recipe, although white asparagus can be quite hard to find outside of Europe. If you do find white asparagus, note that you will want to carefully peel it before steaming, taking careful attention not to break off the tips in the process. This vegan sabayon also goes well with steamed or grilled leeks and endives.

1. Heat the oven to 350°F (180°C). Place the nuts on a baking sheet and bake for 6 to 7 minutes, until lightly toasted. Let cool and then roughly chop.

2. Prepare the sabayon sauce. Pour the soy milk, cider vinegar, mustard, garlic, miso powder, and salt into a blender. Blend until combined. While the blender is running, lift the center cap of the blender and slowly pour in the vegetable oil. You should notice the sauce starting to thicken when about half the oil has been poured in. Continue adding the oil while the blender runs until the oil is blended in. Blend in the lemon juice, salt to taste, and set aside.

3. Break off the woody ends of the asparagus stems. They should break off naturally at the point where they become tender; if not, cut off the last inch (3 cm) of each stem. If the stalks are quite thin, they may even soften up when steaming and need less trimming.

4. Place a steamer basket inside a large pot. Fill it with water until it barely touches the bottom of the steamer basket. Bring to a boil. Add the asparagus and steam until tender, 6 to 8 minutes, depending on the thickness of the stalks. Test the asparagus with a knife; if it slides through easily, then they are done. Remove from the steamer basket to prevent overcooking and immediately rinse with cold water. Spread the asparagus across a serving platter or plate. Allow to either cool completely or serve warm. Spoon the vegan sabayon on top and sprinkle with the chopped nuts, herbed bread crumbs, and fresh herbs.

NOTE: The vegan sabayon can be served at room temperature or slightly warmed. For the latter: Warm it in a saucepan over low heat, stirring constantly for about 1 minute.

Leeks in Vinaigrette with Gribiche and Fried Rosemary

Serves: 2 to 4
Preparation time: 8 minutes
Cooking time: 24 minutes

4 leeks, trimmed (see Note)
2 eggs
1 spring onion, minced
2 tablespoons capers, minced
3 tablespoons Mayonnaise
 (page 40)
1 tablespoon
 stone-ground mustard
1 tablespoon caper brine
3 tablespoons olive oil
2 tablespoons fresh herbs
 (tarragon, chives, or
 others), minced
1 to 2 rosemary sprigs
Sea salt, to taste

Traditionally relegated to the inexpensive, lunchtime preset menu, *poireaux vinaigrette,* which simply means "leeks with vinaigrette," was not always popular. But these days, leeks have been making a comeback.

Not far from my Paris apartment I often have leeks at Brasserie Dubillot—a recent addition to Paris's historically stuffy brasserie scene. So far, this place has got it all right: charming decor, fair prices, and actually friendly waiters (even kid-friendly if I may say so). When I show up with my girlfriends and all our kids, do they complain—surprisingly not! They simply make up a big table for us and we get a little of everything, including a few orders of leeks.

But just because leeks are classic restaurant fare doesn't mean they are difficult to make. They're easy to steam up at home, affordable, and becuase you can steam the leeks in advance, they also make for a great meal to serve a largish gathering (say, all your girlfriends and kids).

1. Prepare the leeks: Cut the leeks crosswise into two or three sections depending on the length of the leek and the size of your cooking pot. Place a steam basket in a large cooking pot and fill with boiling water until it barely touches the basket. Steam the leeks for approximately 15 minutes, or until a sharp knife slides in easily. Remove the leeks from the steaming pot, align them alongside each other on a plate and allow them to cool.

2. Prepare the gribiche: Bring a small pot of water to a boil, gently lower the eggs into the pot, and cook for 8 minutes (less time if your eggs are small and a little more if they're large). Remove the cooked eggs from the pot and rinse them with cold water to stop them from overcooking. Peel the eggs and set them aside.

3. Stir together the spring onions, 1 tablespoon of the capers, the mayonnaise, mustard, caper brine, 1 tablespoon of the olive oil, and the fresh herbs. You shouldn't need to salt the gribiche sauce, as the capers are usually salty enough.

4. Heat the last 2 tablespoons of olive oil in a sauté pan. Clean the rosemary if necessary and make sure to dry it completely; if not it will spatter in the oil. Remove the rosemary leaves from their stems. When the oil is medium hot, but not smoking, gently add the rosemary and let it fry for 1 minute until lightly golden and crispy. Strain the rosemary and reserve the olive oil.

5. To serve: Spread the gribiche sauce over the leeks. Chop the eggs and crumble them on top. Sprinkle with the fried rosemary and the rest of the capers. Pour the reserved rosemary oil on top and sprinkle with sea salt. Enjoy these warm, room temperature, or even cold. You can do as you like, and honestly all will be delicious.

NOTE: To trim your leeks, cut off the bottoms and trim off the leafy green tops. Always be sure to remove the outside layer of the leek, as sometimes dirt and residue can catch in here.

Stuffed Summer Eggplant

Serves: 4 to 6
Preparation time: 30 minutes
Cooking time: 25 minutes

5 small-medium (2½ pounds;
  1 kg) eggplants
⅔ cup (151 ml) milk
1 cup (137 g) minced bread
1¾ cups (200 g) crumbled goat
  cheese or feta
1 cup (227 g) ricotta
1 egg
⅔ cup (67 g) grated
  cheese (Parmesan, white
  Cheddar, Asiago)
½ teaspoon minced garlic
1 teaspoon thyme
2 tablespoons oregano
1 teaspoon salt
¼ cup (21 g) Herbed Bread
  Crumbs (page 27) or
  store-bought
4 tablespoons vegetable oil (I
  like a mix of olive oil, sunflower,
  and other cooking oils)
2 tablespoons XL Herbes de
  Provence (page 22), optional
Lemon juice, for serving

This cheese- and herb-stuffed dish is best made in the South of France in the summer months when eggplants are plentiful. But more often than not, I make it at home in Paris when I'm exhausted and in need of a few vacation days.

1. Bring 1 or 2 large pots of water to a boil. Cut the eggplants in half lengthwise. Boil the eggplants for 10 to 12 minutes each, until a fork easily pierces the flesh, working in batches if necessary. Remove from the boiling water with tongs and let the eggplants cool. Use a paring knife to carefully cut around the edges of the eggplant and a spoon to hollow out the center. The latter should come out rather easily; if not, boil the eggplant another couple minutes. Set aside the hollowed out eggplant skins. Squeeze any excess moisture out of the eggplant flesh, mince, and add the minced eggplant to a large bowl.

2. In a small bowl, pour the milk over the minced bread. Let this rest for a few minutes and then add it to the minced eggplant along with the goat cheese, ricotta, egg, half the grated cheese, the minced garlic, thyme, half the oregano, and salt and toss it all together.

3. Divide the filling among the eggplant skins. Sprinkle with the bread crumbs, the rest of the oregano, and the rest of the shredded cheese. Put the eggplants on a large baking sheet and place in the freezer for 30 minutes—I find this makes them easier to fry afterward, but you can skip this step if you're pressed for time.

4. Heat a tablespoon of the vegetable oil in a large frying pan over medium-hot heat. Add 4 or 5 eggplant halves to the pan (depending on the size) filling side down. While it may seem odd to cook them filling side down, don't worry, it works. You just need to turn them into the pan quickly. Cook for 6 minutes, until the filling makes a dark brown crust. Then, using a large spatula, flip the eggplant halves over to the other side and cook for another 6 minutes. Place the eggplant halves on a baking sheet to rest when done. Working in batches, cook all the eggplant in this manner.

5. You can serve the eggplant at any temperature you like. If serving hot, place the finished eggplant halves in a warm oven while you finish frying the rest. I like to add a little handful of Herbes de Provence on top along with some lemon juice.

Leeks in Vinaigrette with Gribiche and Fried Rosemary

Stuffed Summer Eggplant

Creamy Pumpkin Polenta with Walnut Jam

Serves: 4 to 6
Preparation time: 10 minutes
Cooking time: 30 minutes

1 pound (454 g) pumpkin or
butternut squash
1 tablespoon olive oil
1½ teaspoons sea salt
2 cups (454 ml) whole milk
1 cup (227 ml) water
2 tablespoons butter
½ cup (82 g) polenta
½ cup (160 g) Walnut Jam
(page 44)
¼ cup (25 g) grated Parmesan

The texture of this polenta is not far from that of the creamiest mashed potatoes. I don't bother taking off the skin before blending the pumpkin, as it all combines rather easily. I like to serve this with a poached or sunny-side-up egg.

1. Preheat the oven to 375°F (190° C). Cut the pumpkin in half. Scoop out the seeds and discard. Slice the pumpkin ¾ inch (2 cm) thick. Place the pumpkin slices on a sheet pan, drizzle with the olive oil, and sprinkle with 1 teaspoon of the salt. Roast for 18 to 20 minutes, until tender.

2. Add the roasted pumpkin to a blender with the milk and blend on high speed until smooth. Pour this mixture into a large saucepan over medium-low heat with the water and stir in the butter and the remaining salt. Once the pumpkin mixture is just barely simmering, about 5 minutes, pour in the polenta. Whisk constantly until the polenta is smooth, 4 to 5 minutes. Remove from the heat. Stir in the walnut jam and grate a little Parmesan on top. Serve warm.

Potato Salad with Tzatziki and Fennel

Serves: 4 to 6
Preparation time: 15 minutes
Cooking time: 10 minutes

2 pounds (907 g) small potatoes
(baby red, baby russets,
fingerling), cut into 1-inch
(3 cm) cubes
2 cups (448 g) Seasonal Tzatziki
(page 62)
4 hard-boiled eggs, chopped
1 cup (87 g) diced fennel
¼ cup (61 g) fresh herbs
(chives, parsley, dill, basil)
2 tablespoons lemon juice
1 teaspoon sea salt
1 teaspoon freshly ground
black pepper

I'm sure you know that tzatziki goes well with all kinds of spring and summer raw vegetables. Maybe you're thinking, "But tzatziki isn't French, is it?" And you'd be right: Tzatziki is Greek, though it made its way to Greece from India by way of the Ottoman Empire. This migrating dip is a favorite condiment in France too, as are many yogurt-based sauces and dips. I like to use tzatziki as a replacement for mayonnaise in all sorts of salads, but especially in this potato salad. Feel free to go heavy on the herbs, as the amount and variety make for all the flavor in this salad.

1. Bring a medium-large pot of water to a boil. Boil the potatoes until fork tender, 8 to 10 minutes. Rinse the potatoes in cold water to stop them from overcooking and then let them cool and dry completely.
2. Place the potatoes in a medium salad bowl, stir in the tzatziki, hard-boiled eggs, fennel, herbs, lemon juice, salt, and pepper. Smash the potatoes ever slightly with the back of a fork or a potato masher just to create some starches to help all the flavors combine. Place the potato salad in the refrigerator 30 minutes or up to 2 days before serving.

Crispy Leek and Spinach Tarte with Feta

Serves: 4
Preparation: 10 minutes
Cooking time: 25 minutes

2 tablespoons olive oil

1 leek, trimmed and cut to ½-inch (1 cm) slices

½ garlic clove, minced

10 sheets filo pastry

16 ounces (456 g) feta cheese, diced

8 ounces (226 g) grated mozzarella or Swiss cheese

1 cup (30 g) baby spinach

1 teaspoon oregano

I learned the effortless filo layering trick in this recipe from the wildly popular Parisian chef Cyril Lignac. While a traditional filo pie has layers of filling interspersed with the filo, this recipe uses the filo as a crust. You then just toss whatever kind of vegetable or condiment you'd like on top along with some cheese. This is one of my go-to, ready-in-under-30-minute meals that always impresses. And it's adaptable to whatever you might have left in your fridge— grilled mushrooms and toasted walnuts, homemade Le Pistou (page 34), and sun-dried tomatoes, you name it. Serve with a fresh green salad.

1. Preheat the oven to 375°F (190°C). Heat 1 tablespoon of the olive oil in a nonstick or cast-iron pan and sear the leeks on both sides until golden, 4 to 5 minutes in total. Reserve.

2. Mix together the minced garlic and the remaining olive oil. Brush a sheet of filo pastry with the oil mixture and place it, oiled side down, in a 9-inch (23 cm) springform pan. Continue this process until all the filo is layered one on top of the next. It might look a little messy, and there will definitely be the odd corner sticking out, but no worries.

3. Mix the feta with the mozzarella and sprinkle half of this cheese mixture on top of the filo. Then gently separate the layers of the leek and spread them over the tarte. Add the spinach and sprinkle with the remaining cheese and oregano. Bake for 20 minutes and serve it direct from the oven or at room temperature.

White Bean Hummus and Mushrooms on Toast

Serves: 4
Preparation time: 15 minutes
Cooking time: 10 minutes

FOR THE HUMMUS
1 cup (256 g) tahini paste
½ cup (112 ml) lemon juice
½ cup (100 ml) olive oil
1 teaspoon minced garlic
1 teaspoon cumin powder
¾ teaspoon salt
½ cup (114 ml) warm water
2 cups (358 g) cooked white
  beans (cannellini, navy,
  or butter beans), rinsed
  and drained

FOR THE MUSHROOM TOASTS
½ pound (227 g) mushrooms
  (button, portobello, shiitake),
  cut into ½-inch (1 cm) slices
1 tablespoon olive oil, plus more
  for serving
½ teaspoon garlic powder
Sea salt to taste
8 slices of bread
XL Herbes de Provence
  (page 22)
Toasted Buckwheat (page 29)

This dish is typically something I'd make for an *apéro dînatoire* when my friends, known as the Simones, come over for the evening. It's a kind of single moms with kids club, and they call themselves the Simones after Simone de Beauvoir. It's a really supportive group and we often count on each other for help. But we've all got a lot of kids, and suddenly what starts as an *apéro* ends up spreading itself across most of my plates and bowls and filling up two dishwashers' worth of dishes. *Apéro dinatoire* is more or less the term for that, meaning a laid-back dinner consisting of a variety of appetizers. These toasts are the perfect kind of dish for such an occasion. They come together easily and can obviously be made without mushrooms for slightly picky eaters. I'd suggest using jarred beans, as canned often have a lingering aftertaste.

1. To make the hummus: Blend together in a food processor the tahini paste, lemon juice, ½ cup olive oil, garlic, cumin powder, and salt until it thickens, about 1-2 minutes. Scrape down the sides and blend again until combined. With the food processor running, slowly pour in the warm water. The tahini will become smooth and less compact. Add the beans and blend again until the hummus is smooth, 2 to 3 minutes.

2. Prepare the mushrooms: Make sure your mushrooms are thoroughly dry, as they will cook better and crisp up if they are as dry as possible. I like to press them in between a couple kitchen towels just to make sure I get out as much moisture as possible. Heat a nonstick or cast-iron pan over medium heat. Brush the pan with 1 tablespoon olive oil. Place the mushrooms in the pan and cook for 3 to 4 minutes without stirring. Turn the mushrooms over, sprinkle with the garlic powder and a little salt and cook another 3 minutes, or until they are golden and the edges slightly crispy. Set the mushrooms aside.

3. To make the toasts: Toast the bread and spread generously with the hummus. Top with the mushrooms, a drizzle of olive oil, XL herbes de Provence, toasted buckwheat, and sea salt. Serve right away. Store any leftover hummus in an airtight container in the refrigerator for up to 4 days.

Crispy Leek and Spinach Tarte with Feta

White Bean Hummus and
Mushrooms on Toast

Tomato and Polenta Tarte Tatin

Serves: 4
Preparation time: 10 minutes
Cooking time: 36 minutes

1⅓ pounds (590 g) large
cherry tomatoes or small
Roma tomatoes

1 tablespoon balsamic vinegar

2 tablespoons olive oil

1 tablespoon dried rosemary

½ teaspoon Espelette pepper

½ teaspoon minced garlic

¼ cup (41 g) instant polenta

7 ounces (200 g) premade
puff pastry or the dough from
the Rustic Carrot Tarte with
Burrata and Fennel Dukkah
(page 179)

2 cups (60 g) fresh herbs
and greens (basil, chives,
dill, arugula)

¼ cup (25 g) Parmesan
shavings, optional

This is my ideal end of August recipe. It's the time of year in France when vacation is almost over and thoughts are moving to *la rentrée,* when the cities fill up and buzz with people again, when businesses reopen and school kids prepare for class. It's also when I've had all the tomato salads I can eat and I want something with a little more substance. The tomatoes in this dish are deliciously caramelized yet savory with rosemary and garlic. The polenta absorbs excess tomato juices and helps the pastry crust hold up.

1. Heat the oven to 350°F (180°C). Cut the tomatoes in half and set aside.
2. In a small 8-inch (20 cm) oven-safe frying pan, bring the balsamic vinegar and olive oil to a simmer. When the mixture becomes very bubbly, after about 1 minute, turn off the heat. Sprinkle with the dried rosemary, Espelette pepper, and garlic. Place the tomatoes cut side down, flat against the bottom of the pan. If it seems you have a little too many tomatoes to fit, don't hesitate to really squeeze them in, even if they creep up the side of the pan. Once in the oven they will lose volume and slide down to the bottom of the frying pan.
3. Sprinkle half the polenta on a clean countertop. Roll out the pastry to ½ inch (1 cm) thick. Flip it over, adding the rest of the polenta to the countertop and roll it again so that the polenta has imprinted itself in both sides of the pastry. Find a plate that is slightly larger than the surface of the tomatoes in the bottom of the frying pan. Using the plate as a stencil, place it over the dough and cut around it. Place the cut-out pastry on top of the tomatoes, tucking it in around the edges. Cut a few lines to allow a little air to release from the pastry while the tomatoes cook. Bake for 30 to 35 minutes.
4. Allow the tarte tatin to cool for at least 1 hour and up to 1 night before turning it over. Run a knife around the edges to make sure the tarte is ready to leave the pan. To turn the tarte over, place a cutting board on top with one hand and turn the pan and cutting board over quickly so that you end up with the cutting board on the bottom. Do this over the sink as there might be juices that drip from the pan. Then remove the pan so that the tarte is sitting tomato side up on the cutting board. Slide the tarte onto a plate and cut into slices. Serve the tatin with the fresh herbs and some Parmesan shavings if you like.

Dijon Potato Gratin Pie

Serves: 4 to 6
Preparation time: 20 minutes
Cooking time: 1 hour
25 minutes

2 pounds (2 pounds; 1 kg)
   russet potatoes
2 tablespoons butter
2 tablespoons flour
2 cups (454 ml) whole milk
1½ cups (150 g) grated cheese
   (Parmesan, sharp Cheddar,
   Gruyère, Swiss, provolone)
1 garlic clove, minced
½ teaspoon nutmeg
2 tablespoons Dijon mustard
1 teaspoon salt
1 teaspoon fresh ground pepper,
   black or white
2 puff pastry sheets
1 egg yolk
Fleur de sel or sea salt

You can serve this potato pie as a side dish, or you can present it as a meal in itself with a green salad. When it comes to making béchamel sauces, I often just grate up whatever cheese bits and leftovers I might have at hand, as I often find the more varieties the merrier.

1. Preheat oven to 350°F (180°C).
2. Wash and dry the potatoes; it's not necessary to peel them but you can if you like. Slice them as thinly as possible, ideally with a mandolin, ⅛ inch thick.
3. Make the béchamel sauce: Melt the butter in a medium saucepan. Add the flour and whisk until combined and clumpy, about 2 minutes. Slowly pour in the milk, whisking constantly. As the milk heats up, the sauce will begin to thicken, 3 to 4 minutes. When this happens, turn off the heat and add the grated cheese little by little, whisking constantly. Stir in the garlic, nutmeg, mustard, salt, and pepper.
4. Place 1 sheet of puff pastry in a lightly buttered deep dish pie pan or circular springform pan; prick the puff pastry all over with a fork. Spread a third of the sliced potatoes across the pan. Pour one-third of the béchamel on top. Repeat two more times with the potatoes and béchamel sauce. Place the second puff pastry on top. Fold the edges together to close into a rustic crust. Slice four 2-inch (5 cm) incisions across the crust. Whisk the egg yolk and brush it over the crust. Bake for 40 minutes, or until the crust is golden brown. Sprinkle with fleur de sel. Cover with aluminum foil to prevent overcooking and bake for another 40 minutes. Let the potato gratin rest for 20 to 30 minutes before serving.

NOTE: This recipe is almost even better reheated the next day at 325°F (160°C). Cover with aluminum foil while reheating.

Cauliflower, Carrot, and Parsnip Parmentier Pie

Serves: 4
Preparation time: 25 minutes
Cooking time: 50 minutes

⅔ pound (300 g) parsnips, peeled and cut into 1-inch (3 cm) pieces

1⅓ pounds (603 g) cauliflower, cut into 1-inch (3 cm) pieces

2 tablespoons (25 g) butter

½ cup (57 g) grated cheese

½ garlic clove, minced

½ teaspoon sea salt

2 tablespoons olive oil

3 carrots, chopped

2 celery stalks, minced

1 onion, minced

1 tablespoon Herbed Bread Crumbs (page 27)

Parmentier, which was said to have been served to Louis XVI, is a meaty casserole known for its creamy mashed potato topping. For a less royalist (and vegetarian) version, I like to use cauliflower and parsnips—celery root or butternut squash can also be substituted for the latter, but I suggest always keeping the cauliflower for the creaminess it brings. This is also one of those dishes that, as long as you follow the proportions, is great for using up any type of leftover sautéed vegetable for its filling. Serve with a salad on the side.

1. Preheat the oven to 350°F (180°C). Bring a large pot of water to a boil. Add the parsnips and cauliflower and cook for 10 to 12 minutes, until the vegetables are tender. Drain the water and press the vegetables with a spatula in a colander to remove as much water as possible. Add the cauliflower and parsnips to a blender or food processor with the butter, cheese, garlic, and salt and blend until smooth.

2. Heat the olive oil over medium-low heat in a large frying pan. Sauté the carrots, celery, and onions for 10 minutes, or until slightly tender. Spread this mixture over the bottom of an 8-by-12-inch (15-by-30 cm) rectangular baking dish and spread the parsnip-cauliflower puree on top. Sprinkle with the bread crumbs and bake until golden, 25 to 28 minutes. Serve hot.

Mushroom and Potato Tartiflette

Serves: 4 to 6
Preparation time: 15 minutes
Cooking time: 54 minutes

10 small potatoes, such as
 Russet or Yukon
3 (½ pound; 227 g)
 portobello mushrooms
3 tablespoons olive oil
1 small white onion, sliced
1 garlic clove, minced
1 tablespoon
 stone-ground mustard
½ teaspoon salt
1 cup (227 ml) cream
8 ounces (225 g) Camembert

This is the best gateway cheese dish for anyone. And yes, I mean anyone, even for those who don't like stinky cheese or have a dislike of cheese rinds. When this cheese casserole arrives on the table everyone will have a joke about how much certain cheeses stink. But once they taste the melted Camembert . . . it's another story. The sharpness is balanced out by the cooking time as well as the potatoes and mushrooms, resulting in a guaranteed crowd pleaser. Seeing as the sauce in this dish is quite rich, you can serve it with salad greens to balance things out. You probably won't need a vinaigrette dressing, however. It might also be good to have a little bread on hand for cleaning off the plates at the end.

1. Clean and scrub the potatoes. You can choose to leave the skins on or you can peel them; it's up to you. Place a steamer basket in a medium pot with a fitted lid. Fill the bottom with boiling water until it barely touches the steam basket—as you want to be careful not to boil the potatoes. Cover and steam the potatoes for 15 minutes until a knife passes easily through the potato. Remove the potatoes from the steamer basket and slice them ¼ inch (½ cm) thick.
2. Preheat the oven to 350°F (180°C).
3. Wash and dry the mushrooms. I like to press them in between two kitchen towels to absorb as much moisture as possible, as this will help them cook better in the oven. Slice the mushrooms ½ inch (1 cm) thick. Heat half the olive oil in a sauté pan over medium heat. Add the mushrooms and sauté for 3 to 4 minutes, until lightly browned. Turn over the mushrooms, add the rest of the olive oil and the onions, and cook for another 4 minutes. Add the garlic and cook for another minute, stirring frequently. Turn off the heat and stir in the mustard, salt, and cream. Stir in the potatoes.
4. Pour the mushroom and potato mixture into a deep, oven-safe 8-by-10-inch (20-by-25 cm) baking dish. Cut the Camembert in half lengthwise to make two circles with the rind on the outside of each. Cut each circle into triangles and place them on top of the potatoes, rind side up. Place in the oven and bake for 25 to 30 minutes until golden brown on top.

Smoky Lentil Stew with Scamorza

Serves: 4
Preparation time: 20 minutes
Cooking time: 50 minutes

2 tablespoons olive oil

1 onion, diced

2 carrots, diced

1 garlic clove, minced

1 cup (198 g) green or
brown lentils

2 teaspoons cumin powder

2 teaspoons smoked paprika

2 teaspoons dried thyme

1 teaspoon dried rosemary

One 14-ounce can
diced tomatoes

1 teaspoon salt

7 cups (1½ L) water

8 ounces (228 g) smoked
scamorza, grated (see Note)

Scattered along the French-Italian border are rustic mountain refuges. Access to these remote Alpine lodges is only by hiking boot (or backwoods skis). I can attest that the hike itself is magnificent, and wild flowers abound almost under every step. Streams of cold mountain water rush under rustic bridges. It's so awe inspiring that I don't even think about what I'm going to eat next. Last autumn I hiked out to one such refuge. I didn't really have any expectations about the food, which is delivered in bulk quantities every month. But after a five-hour hike I sat down to a piping hot plat du jour that, like this recipe, blended French village cuisine with melty Italian cheeses. The sunset on the Italian Alps wasn't too bad either—a meal well worth the effort! I suggest serving this Alpine stew with a generous spoon of creamy polenta, or just on its own with a hunk of rustic bread.

1. Heat the olive oil in a Dutch oven or pot over medium-low heat. Add the onions and carrots and sauté for 5 minutes. Then add the garlic along with the lentils, spices, dried herbs, tomatoes, salt, and water. Let simmer uncovered for 45 minutes. Remove approximately 1 cup of the stew and blend it smooth in a blender or with an immersion blender. Add the blended mixture back to the stew, adding a little more water if the stew seems too thick, or if you would like your final result to be more like a soup.

2. Stir half of the smoked scamorza into the stew. Then serve piping hot, along with the rest of the smoked scamorza.

NOTE: If you can't find scamorza, don't hesitate to replace it with another grateable cheese like Comté, Cheddar, or even Fontina.

Celery Root Soup Done "French Onion" Style

Serves: 2
Preparation time: 10 minutes
Cooking time: 30 minutes

⅔ pound (300 g) celery
   root, peeled
5 cups (1.2 L) miso broth
1 tablespoon butter or olive oil
1 medium yellow or white onion,
   thinly sliced
1 teaspoon minced garlic
1 teaspoon thyme
1 tablespoon soy sauce
Sea salt to taste
2 cups (224 g) toasted bread
   cubes or Croutons (page 27)
½ cup (57 g) grated cheese
   (Comté, Emmental,
   Gruyère, Cheddar)
1 tablespoon minced chives

French onion soup has an unfortunate reputation for being heavy and laden with butter. I wanted to come up with a lighter recipe that could be made with olive oil or other vegetables, and would be easier to digest. The version I created was just as good as the 2 AM version I first tasted at Saint Michel as a student. A traditional *soupe à l'oignon gratiné* not only kept you warm as you made your way home after the last metro had closed, it was a common antidote for students after a night out. Now I make it at home and use celery root or parsnip with broiled cheese or "gratiné." It strikes just the right balance of healthy and indulgent that I'm always looking for in the winter months.

1. Slice the celery root in a julienne or grate it on a large grade in a food processor or with a four-sided grater.
2. Melt the butter in a large sauté pan. Add the onion, celery root, garlic, and thyme. Lightly cook over medium low-heat for 15 minutes. It's okay if the edges of the vegetables brown, but only just slightly. Pour in the soy sauce to deglaze the mixture and scrape up any browned bits from the bottom of the pan. Heat the miso broth over low heat in a medium saucepan for 5 minutes.
3. Add the celery root and onion mixture to the miso broth and add salt to taste. Depending on the miso you use, you might not need any salt at all. Simmer for 10 minutes and then divide the hot soup between two generous bowls or four smaller bowls. If you plan to gratiné the cheese, make sure these are oven-safe bowls. Stir in the toasted bread cubes and sprinkle the cheese on top.
4. You can either serve as such, with the cheese melting as you stir it into the soup, or you can gratiné the cheese, which means to more or less broil the cheese in order to get a crispy, gooey topping. There are two different ways to do this: either heat up your broiler on medium and place the oven-safe bowls beneath it for 3 to 4 minutes, or use a handheld kitchen torch to melt and brown the cheese. Sprinkle with chives and serve immediately.

Pistou Brioche Buns

Makes: 12 buns
Preparation time: 25 minutes
Cooking time: 22 minutes
Rest time: 2½ hours

2½ cups (300 g) flour,
    more if needed
1 tablespoon sugar
2 teaspoon active dry yeast
3 eggs
1 teaspoon salt
¼ cup (57 ml) warm water
6 tablespoons butter, cubed,
    room temperature, plus more
    for greasing
¾ cup (100 g) Le Pistou
    (page 34)

Brioche is best made over long weekends and rainy afternoons. It's then that you can really enjoy the scent as it cooks in your oven. The buns are good on their own, but I always like to add a little something inside—if it's not pistou (French style pesto), it might be some tapenade or simply some chopped olives and dried rosemary.

1. Stir together the flour, sugar, and yeast in an electric stand mixer with a paddle attachment. Add 2 of the eggs, the salt and the warm water and knead for 10 minutes with a hook attachment on low speed. Add the butter cubes, little by little, mixing well between each addition. Mix until the dough is soft and smooth, 10 to 12 minutes. The dough should be quite humid. If the dough is sticky and doesn't come together into a ball, add in a tablespoon of flour and mix for another minute. Remove the dough and place it in a lightly oiled bowl covered with a towel until the dough has doubled in size, approximately 1 hour.

2. Punch down the dough and roll it into a rectangle, approximately 8 by 10 inches (15 by 25 cm). Spread the pistou across the dough, all the way to the edges. Roll the dough upward into a long cylinder. Set the dough on a cutting board or plate and place in the refrigerator for 10 minutes. Cut the dough into 16 equal parts. Place them on a lightly buttered 10-inch (25 cm) square baking pan, one next to the other. Cover with a towel and let rise for 1½ hours.

3. Preheat the oven to 375°F (180°F). Beat the additional egg and brush it over the buns. Bake for 20 to 22 minutes, until slightly golden. Serve immediately. The brioche buns will keep for 2 days in an airtight container. Reheat for 5 minutes in a warm oven.

Celery Root Soup Done "French Onion" Style

Pistou Brioche Buns

MAIN DISHES

That Are Meant to Share

5

In France there are small plates to share, and I'm a big fan of those—eaten at my counter with friends—but sometimes I need a *plat de résistance,* the kind of dish that gives me an excuse to pull out my oversized serving plates from the flea market and my best mismatched cloth napkins.

These are weekend recipes, dishes meant to encourage lingering at the table. These aren't mains to rush through eating. Yet many come together quickly or can be made ahead. This gives you the time you need to organize the essentials: stack up the plates, choose the glasses, and open a couple bottles of wine. A little advance table prep means you get more time at the table because you won't be dashing back for more of this or that.

I also always make sure I have good bread on hand. This chapter has many recipes *en sauce,* so you simply cannot neglect the bread. For me, sometimes this is even more important than serving several courses or even a dessert—because good bread draws out the meal, makes it last. It doesn't have to be baguette, just something with a little crunch on the outside and tender enough inside for mopping up whatever might be left.

Winter Vegetable Bourguignon Stew

Serves: 4
Preparation time: 25 minutes
Cooking time: 1 hour
23 minutes

2 tablespoons butter

1 small yellow onion, thinly sliced

1 garlic clove, minced

2 tablespoons flour

2 cups (454 ml) hot water

3 cups (708 ml) red wine
(Burgundy, Pinot Noir,
Beaujolais, Touraine)

3 medium sized carrots, peeled
and roughly chopped

2 small turnips, roughly chopped

½ of a small celery root, peeled
and roughly chopped

1 leek, trimmed and chopped
into 1-inch (3 cm) pieces

1 teaspoon miso paste

1 tablespoon soy sauce

1 tablespoon sesame oil

1 teaspoon sea salt

3 cups (234 g) thickly
sliced mushrooms, ¾ inch
(2 cm) thick

1 tablespoon vegetable oil
(canola, grapeseed)

Fresh black pepper for serving

Stone-ground mustard
for serving

This is really the meal for warming up a cold house on a winter's night; it involves a good amount of chopping to warm up your body and it simmers just long enough to warm up a cold kitchen while you get a good fire going in the fireplace. This recipe takes inspiration from two classic French stews: pot-au-feu and boeuf bourguignon, both of which have red meat in them but also lots of vegetables. Feel free to substitute different root or winter vegetables such as parsnips or rutabaga, but don't leave out the turnips or the mushrooms! Along with the miso paste and soy sauce, they bring out a lot of umami rich flavor.

I like to serve this velvety stew with an indulgent purée (such as potato, celery root, cauliflower, or a mixture of all three) or with a potato gratin, like Dijon Potato Gratin Pie (page 156). For an accompaniment, choose a decent red wine. It doesn't have to be a burgundy (or even French!), just make sure it's not too heavy or overly tannic. Eaten right next to the fireplace at my boyfriend's house in Nantes, this is my quintessential winter's meal.

1. Melt the butter over medium-low heat in a large cast-iron pot. Add the onion and garlic and lightly brown for about 5 minutes. Stirring quickly, add the flour and continue stirring until it is fully combined to make a roux. Pour in the hot water and stir with a whisk until the roux is dissolved, about 2 minutes. Add the wine along with the carrots, turnips, celery root, and leeks. Add the miso paste, soy sauce, sesame oil, and salt. Bring to a boil and then simmer for 40 minutes.

2. In the meantime, prepare the mushrooms. Heat the vegetable oil in a large frying pan until shimmering and then add the mushrooms. Allow the mushrooms to brown for at least 3 minutes over medium heat before turning and browning again on the other side. Add them to the stew and simmer for another 30 minutes. Serve the stew in shallow bowls with a little cracked black pepper and stone-ground mustard on the side.

North African Vegetable Stew

Serves: 4
Preparation time: 15 minutes
Cooking time: 55 minutes

2 tablespoons olive oil

1 large onion, thinly sliced

1 garlic clove, thinly sliced

1 large tomato, diced

1 pound (450 g) carrots, peeled and cut into 1½-inch (4 cm) pieces

1 pound (450 g) potatoes, peeled and cut into 1½-inch (4 cm) pieces

1 pound (450 g) turnips, peeled and cut into 1½-inch (4 cm) pieces

6 cups (1½ L) water

1 teaspoon salt

1 tablespoon ras el hanout Moroccan spice

⅔ pound (300 g) zucchini, cut into 1½-inch (4 cm) slices

10 ounces (285 g) canned chickpeas

Red Pepper Harissa (page 39)

Just next to the visual arts school I attended in the 11ème arrondissement was a small Moroccan restaurant. It was there that I was introduced to the warm spices and stew of North African cuisine. Two or three of my friends and I would share a pot of the 7€ vegetable stew. It was served next to a large silver platter of couscous—often refilled at least once by the owner himself. He showed us the ceremony of stirring a small spoon of harissa in a ladle of broth before pouring it in our plate, and he would serve extra chickpeas on the side. The restaurant didn't survive the restaurant gentrification of the neighborhood, but the generosity of the stew has stayed with me. It's the kind of stew I make when I know there will be at least four at the table, but I often double the recipe just in case someone needs an extra helping or two. I like to serve the vegetables cut to larger sizes. This means we have to take the time to cut them on the plate, because this is the kind of meal that should be served hot and eaten slowly. Serve on its own as a stew or over fluffy couscous.

1. Heat the olive oil in a large pot over medium-low heat. Add the onions, garlic, and tomato and sauté for 5 minutes. Add the carrots, potatoes, and turnips to the pot, along with the water, salt, and ras el hanout spice. Simmer for 35 minutes. Add the zucchini and chickpeas to the pot. If the water doesn't sufficiently cover all the vegetables, add another cup. Simmer for another 15 minutes. Serve with red pepper harissa.

Pistou Stew with Seasonal Greens and White Beans

Serves: 4
Preparation time: 15 minutes
Cooking time: 50 minutes

2 tablespoons olive oil
½ cup (71 g) minced onion
1 tablespoon rosemary,
   fresh or dried
1 teaspoon thyme
3 cups (681 ml) water
1 cup (90 g) carrots,
   peeled and diced
1 cup (90 g) green beans,
   chopped in 1-inch
   (3 cm) pieces
2 cups (140 g) broccoli, diced
1 cup (90 g) zucchini, diced
1½ cups (225 g) cooked and
   drained white beans (navy
   or cannellini)
1 teaspoon salt
¾ cup (100 g) Le Pistou
   (page 34)

Compared to school lunches in the cafeterias of the States, lunch for French school kids is practically fine dining. School lunches are four-course meals, nutritionally balanced and carefully composed to include a starter, main, cheese course, and dessert. Almost all the produce is seasonal, often organic, and comes from France. School children eat vegetarian meals twice a week and many even have the option of doing so every day. It also happens to be affordable, as families pay on a sliding scale based on their earnings. As luck would have it, I ended up consulting for the national school lunch menu, and now some of my recipes are served to kids—including my own daughters—in public schools every week in France. This stew served as inspiration for one of the recipes I created for the school menu. It combines vegetables that most children already know, like carrots and broccoli, and associates them with new flavors such as rosemary and thyme. So when you eat this recipe you'll know that it has been tested and approved by thousands of French school children.

1. Heat the olive oil in a medium-large pot over low heat. Add the onion, rosemary, and thyme and gently sauté without browning, for 5 minutes. Add the water, carrots, green beans, and broccoli and bring to a boil. Then reduce the heat to a simmer and cook for 30 minutes. Add the zucchini, beans, and salt and simmer for another 15 minutes. Divide the soup among four bowls and add a spoon of pistou to each just before serving.

NOTE: What I especially like to do when I have leftover soup, and what I did for the school lunches in France, was to blend two-thirds of the soup into a smooth sauce and serve it over pasta with the remaining stew. So, that being said, you may just want to double up the ingredients when you make this recipe.

Spring Vegetable Tarte

Serves: 4
Preparation time: 15 minutes
Cooking time: 28 minutes

6 asparagus stalks

5 ounces (140 g) Pâte Feuilleté
(page 71) or puff pastry

1 egg

2 tablespoons crème fraîche or
sour cream

½ cup (50 g) plus 1 tablespoon
shredded cheese (Parmesan,
mozzarella, white Cheddar, feta)

¾ cup (177 g) canned and
marinated artichokes, chopped

⅔ cup (96 g) peas (fresh
or frozen)

Fresh herbs and/or spring
greens (such as mesclun)
for serving

You can use pretty much any type of tender spring veggies in this recipe, like peas and asparagus, or in the summer months yellow squash and eggplant. Sometimes I make Artichokes à la Barigoule, artichokes braised in white wine (page 114), just to make this spring veggie tarte. And a note about artichokes for this dish: If you do not want to braise your own artichokes, canned and marinated artichokes are just fine!

1. Preheat the oven to 350°F (180°C).
2. Bring a medium sized pot of water to a boil. Wash and trim the asparagus, removing the hard bottom part of the stalk. Cut in half. Blanch for 1 minute in boiling water, or 2 minutes if the stalks are thicker.
3. Roll out the pâte feuilleté or puff pastry into an 8-by-10 inch (20-by-25 cm) rectangle. Place it on a parchment-lined or lightly oiled baking sheet. Fold the sides in to form a narrow crust. Whisk together the egg with the crème fraîche or sour cream and the ½ cup of the shredded cheese. Spread this over the pâte feuilleté or puff pastry up until the folded edge and then cover with the artichokes, asparagus, and peas. Bake for 25 minutes or until the edges are golden. Let the tarte cool to room temperature and serve with fresh herbs and/or spring greens tossed right on top and the remaining 1 tablespoon of the grated cheese.

Rustic Carrot Tarte with Burrata and Fennel Dukkah

Serves: 4
Preparation time: 20 minutes
Cooking time: 35 minutes

RUSTIC DOUGH

½ cup (113 g) cold butter
2 cups (240 g) flour
1 egg
2 tablespoons water
1 teaspoon salt

4 medium (about ¾ pound;
   340 g) carrots, peeled
   and shaved
1 small (125 g) fennel bulb,
   thinly sliced
2 tablespoons olive oil
¼ cup (25 g) grated Parmesan
1 egg white, lightly beaten
8 ounces (226 g) burrata
Fennel leaves or other
   greens or herbs
2 tablespoons Fennel Hazelnut
   Dukkah (page 25)

A colorful, winter vegetable tarte—*mais oui!* When I want something convivial that can be made ahead and served anytime from brunch to lunch to apéro or dinner, I often turn to these rustic tartes. And if you're looking for extra comfort, double up on the cheese or spread on a little Green Olive Tapenade (page 58).

1. Cut the butter into small ½-inch (1 cm) cubes and place it with the flour in the bowl of a stand mixer with the whisk attachment. Beat for approximately 3 minutes until a crumbly homogenous mixture. Add the egg, water, and ½ teaspoon of the salt. Switch the whisk for a pastry hook and beat again until a smooth ball forms, about 2 minutes. Place the dough in the refrigerator while you prepare the vegetables.

2. In a large bowl, mix together the carrots and fennel with the olive oil, Parmesan, and remaining salt.

3. Preheat the oven to 350°F (180°C) and lightly oil a baking sheet. Remove the crust from the refrigerator and knead it for a few minutes on a lightly floured surface. Roll it out into a circle, approximately 12 to 14 inches (30 to 36 cm) wide and ¼ to ½ inch (½ to 1 cm) thick. Lift the dough onto the baking sheet and place the carrot and fennel mixture in the center. Pull the remaining sides of the dough up over the edges of the vegetables to hold them in place. The resulting tarte should be about 10 inches (25 cm) in diameter. Brush the sides of the dough with the egg white. Bake for 30 to 35 minutes, until the edges are golden. Let the tarte cool for at least 30 minutes or up to 2 days before serving. Serve with the burrata, fennel leaves, and fennel dukkah.

NOTE: You can also prepare the crust by hand. In a medium bowl, crumble the flour and cubed butter with your fingers until the mixture is homogenous. Then create a well in the center, add the egg and water, and hand knead for 5 minutes until a smooth dough forms.

Spring Vegetable Tarte

Rustic Carrot Tarte with Burrata
and Fennel Dukkah

Leftover Bottle of Red Wine Risotto

Serves: 2 to 4
Preparation time: 15 minutes
Cooking time: 41 minutes

1 cup (227 ml) vegetable or
    miso broth
2½ cups (587 ml) red wine
2 tablespoons butter
1 small onion, minced
½ teaspoon minced garlic
1 cup (8 ounces; 225 g)
    Arborio rice
1 cup (100 g) Parmesan cheese,
    grated, plus more for serving
Sea salt
1 handful flat-leaf parsley
Freshly ground black pepper

This recipe is ideal for those nights when your wine cellar is better stocked than your fridge. The deep burgundy hue of this risotto begs for candlelight. It works well with white wine too, but the visual effect just isn't the same! This is the kind of recipe that wafts through the winter air. It once had my neighbors asking, "What was it that you made for dinner last night that smelled so delicious . . . ?!"

1. Heat the broth and red wine together in a large saucepan over low heat until warm.
2. Melt the butter in a wide saucepan or Dutch oven. Add the onion and garlic and cook until translucent, approximately 6 minutes, stirring frequently. Stir in the rice and cook for 5 minutes, stir often so that the rice does not stick. Begin adding the warm wine-miso broth little by little, stirring after each addition until completely absorbed. This process will take approximately 30 minutes to add all the broth. Stir in the Parmesan and salt to taste. Divide the risotto among the plates, dress with the parsley, and serve with more Parmesan and fresh ground black pepper.

NOTE: Sometimes I double this recipe just to have enough leftover risotto to make something like arancini the next day. I just form the risotto into balls, stuff them with Comté or mozzarella cheese, and fry them up. They undoubtedly should be served with a glass of red wine at apéro time.

Spring Provençal Risotto

Serves: 4
Preparation time: 20 minutes
Cooking time: 41 minutes

3½ cups (830 ml) broth from
  Artichoke à la Barigoule
  (page 114), or vegetable broth
  or light miso
1½ cups (355 g) artichokes
  (steamed and trimmed
  or jarred)
2 tablespoons butter
1 small white onion, minced
1 cup (225 g) risotto rice
⅔ cup (156 ml) white wine
4 stalks green asparagus
2 carrots, peeled and sliced
½ cup (73 g) peas
½ cup (50 g) grated Parmesan
  cheese for serving, optional

It comes as no surprise that the country that created the Michelin rating system as well as the brigade kitchen hierarchy of chef, sous-chef, chef de partie—and which peels even the smallest of potatoes—has a reputation for taking itself seriously. Yet the rigor is a little more relaxed in some parts of the country, especially in the South and Provence region of France. In my opinion, this is due to the melting pot of food cultures from Italy, Spain, and North Africa that blend easily into the menus of local restaurants.

The broth for this recipe is quite adaptable. You can either use the recipe for Artichokes à la Barigoule (page 114) to create the broth, or you can substitute with a vegetable broth or a light miso broth. No matter what broth you use, the secret for this soup base is to blend in half a cup of artichokes. This will infuse your rice grains with extra artichoke flavor.

1. Prepare your broth by blending it with ½ cup of the artichokes, either in a blender of with an immersion blender. Add this mixture to a medium saucepan and bring it to a simmer. Meanwhile, melt the butter in a medium-large saucepan with high sides. Add the onions and cook until they are translucent, about 6 minutes. Pour in the rice and sauté for 5 minutes. Pour in the white wine and stir until it is completely absorbed by the rice. Then begin to add the broth little by little, stirring frequently with each addition until it is absorbed by the rice. This process should take about 30 minutes.
2. Prepare the vegetables: Break off the stems from the asparagus and chop into 2- to 3-inch (5 to 8 cm) pieces. Add the carrots during the last 15 minutes of cooking time and the asparagus and peas during the last 10 minutes of cooking time. Serve with the Parmesan cheese or as it is.

Smoked Tea and Mushroom Risotto

Serves: 4 to 6
Preparation time: 15 minutes
Cooking time: 51 minutes
Rest time: 1 hour

2 bags black tea (preferably
Lapsang Souchong
smoked tea)
4 cups (1 L) boiling water
2 tablespoons miso powder
1 teaspoon salt
1 pound (454 g)
mushrooms (portobello,
cremini, chanterelles)
4 tablespoons butter
2 tablespoons olive oil
1 small onion, minced
1 garlic clove, minced
1⅓ cups (250 g) risotta rice
(arborio or carnaroli)
½ cup (120 ml) beer or
white wine
⅔ cup (67 g) grated
Parmesan cheese
Salt
Black pepper

Last winter, my boyfriend and I stayed at a rental cottage just outside of Marseille, one of the warmest places year-round in France. On one particular evening though, it was freezing and windy. We only had a wood-burning stove, and it was kind of rustic—the place was held up with metal beams, because the structure was shot. It belonged to the owner of a small restaurant in town. It was gorgeous although completely falling apart—I guess that was what made it so charming. We still hadn't figured out how to get a fire started and I was wearing my coat inside the kitchen as I was cooking. I had already started making mushrooms for a risotto when I realized I didn't have much for a broth. We had been traveling for a few days already, and fortunately I had grabbed some dry goods from the kitchen of my boyfriend's family apartment (where we had stayed a couple days before) to get us settled into our rental. Going out into the chill of the night meant taking a manual transmission car up a steep hill in the dark, so I was determined to say put and use what we had on hand. Luckily, despite a lack of broth, I had taken some instant miso powder and two bags of Chinese smoked tea. The risotto turned out wonderfully. Now when I want a quick and earthy broth, this is the one I make to remind me of that chilly Marseille night.

1. Steep the tea in the boiling water off of the heat for 5 minutes. Stir in the miso powder and the salt. Clean and trim the mushrooms. Slice the mushrooms rather thickly. Melt half the butter and all the olive oil together in a sauté pan. Add the mushrooms and sauté over medium-high heat for 4 to 5 minutes on each side. If your sauté pan isn't big enough to cook them all comfortably, use two pans or cook them in batches. Remove the mushrooms from the heat, mince half of them, and set aside the rest. Add the minced mushrooms and the miso-tea broth to a blender and give it a few pulses, just to give the broth more flavor while leaving some of the mushroom texture.

2. Melt the rest of the butter in a large sauté pan or braiser and gently sauté the onion and garlic together for 6 minutes over low heat. Add the rice and sauté for another 5 minutes, stirring frequently. Pour in the beer and continue stirring until the liquid is fully absorbed into the rice. Then little by little, add the miso-tea broth and stir with each addition until the liquid is completely absorbed by the rice. This process will take about 30 minutes. Stir in the rest of the mushrooms and half the Parmesan. Season with salt and pepper to taste. Serve with the rest of the Parmesan.

Spring Provençal Risotto

BOHÈME COOKING

Smoked Tea and Mushroom Risotto

Mini Ravioli (de Royans) with Greens and Cheese

Serves: 4 to 6
Preparation time: 1 hour
Rest time: 2 hours
Cooking time: 10 to 13 minutes

FOR THE RAVIOLI FILLING

½ cup (113 g) butter
2 cups (122 g) packed greens
   (parsley, basil, spinach,
   arugula), minced
1¼ cups (141 g) shredded
   cheese (I like to use a mix of
   2 or 3 white cheeses)
2 egg yolks
1 teaspoon salt

FOR THE PASTA

4 eggs
1 tablespoon water
3½ cups (420 g) flour
½ teaspoon salt

TO SERVE

Butter
Olive oil
Grated Parmesan cheese

Ravioli is one of my youngest daughter's favorite foods, and we just recently learned how to make them ourselves. Contrary to most ravioli, this French specialty from the Alps is served with the ravioli sheets left whole. There are many ways to serve them: simply boiled for 3 minutes and dressed with butter and grated cheese, pan-fried with sage and olive oil for a richer dish, or baked in the oven with a little béchamel for a gratin style pasta. For the last two preparations you will need to parboil the ravioli for 2 minutes. No matter how you prepare your ravioli, take care not to overcook the pasta and be sure to remove them from the water gently with a sieve so as not to break the sheets. Traditionally the cheese filling is seasoned with parsley or spinach, but I like to use both and also add in some greens like arugula and basil.

1. To make the ravioli filling, melt the butter in a medium saucepan. Add the greens and cook over low heat until they are completely wilted, about 4 minutes. Remove the pan from the heat and let cool. Add the cheese, egg yolks, and salt. Stir together to combine and then place in the refrigerator for at least 3 hours.

2. In the meantime, prepare the pasta dough. Break the eggs into a 1 cup measuring cup. The eggs won't completely fill the cup. Add the tablespoon of water and a little extra if necessary to fill the cup, then set this aside.

3. Add the flour and salt to a medium bowl and mix them together. Then, using either your hands or a stand mixer (with a dough hook), incorporate the eggs little by little until a dough forms. Knead by hand for 10 minutes or in a mixer for 3 minutes at speed 2 until the dough is smooth. Form the dough into a round ball and place in a lightly oiled bowl. Let the dough rest for 30 minutes. The dough will expand just slightly.

4. Divide the dough into six parts. On a lightly floured surface, roll out one of your dough pieces into an oblong disk and flatten as much as possible. Feed the dough into a pasta maker set at a low setting of either 1 or 2. Feed the dough through the machine two times. Then adjust the grade to 4 and feed the dough through again. Adjust the grade to 5 and feed the dough through one more time. The final sheet of pasta should be roughly the width of a single ravioli mold and double the length of a ravioli mold in order to account for the bottom and top layers. Place the dough on a lightly floured surface and follow the same process with the rest of the dough, making sure that each sheet of pasta is about the same width and length for your mold.

5. Place a sheet of pasta on the ravioli mold. Situate the pasta sheet so that half of it is on the ravioli mold and half is hanging off the mold. You will fold this unused portion of the dough back over the other to seal the ravioli. Push the pasta down into the squares of your mold. Then fill each square with a little filling, about ½ teaspoon—a pastry bag works well, as do your fingers and a teaspoon. Once all the squares are filled, fold the unused half of the pasta sheet on top, centering the pasta so that it closes on all sides. Seal the ravioli by pressing firmly on top with a rolling pin, taking care not to press too hard and separate each ravioli square. Remove the sheet of ravioli, place on a lightly floured surface and proceed with the rest of the pasta sheets in this manner.

6. Bring a large pot of salted water to a boil. Cook the ravioli in batches for 3 minutes, being careful not to overcrowd the pot as you go. When the 3 minutes are up, remove each batch of ravioli delicately with a skimmer. Serve with butter and/or olive oil and grated Parmesan cheese.

NOTE: You will need a pasta laminator for this recipe, as the pasta sheets need to be quite thin. In addition, you will need a ravioli mold. Sounds kind of equipment heavy I know, but I have to say that making my own pasta is one of the most joyful moments I have in the kitchen with my daughters. It doesn't take long to get the hang of pulling the pasta sheets, and the process in itself is very rewarding, not to mention that the results are delicious. I use a 4-by-10-inch (10-by-25 cm) ravioli mold (48 mini raviolis).

Mini Ravioli (de Royans)
with Greens and Cheese

BOHÈME COOKING

Buckwheat Mountain Pasta

Makes: About 2 pounds
(907 g) fresh pasta
Preparation time: 35 minutes
Cooking time: 3 minutes

FOR THE PASTA
2⅓ cups (280 g) buckwheat
   flour, plus more for dusting
1⅓ cups (160 g) white flour
2 large eggs
¾ cup (170 ml) hot water
1 tablespoon salt

FOR SERVING
Extra virgin olive oil
Butter or cream
Cheese (grated Comté,
   Cheddar, Parmesan)

People assume that France doesn't have its own pasta tradition. But crozets, which are mini squares of buckwheat pasta, are typical in the mountains year-round. You can make this dish without a pasta maker, although you can use one if you prefer. Just make sure both your eggs and flour are room temperature before making this recipe.

I like to eat crozets quite simply, but sometimes after boiling I will stir in some sautéed leeks, cream, shredded Gruyère, and bake in the oven for 20 minutes. This hearty baked version is especially appreciated after a day in the cold.

1. Mix together the flours in a stand mixer or with a whisk. In a small bowl, whisk the eggs together and pour in the hot water. The water should be hot to the touch, but not burning. Set up the stand mixer with the dough hook attachment. Add the salt and pour the liquid mixture into the bowl of the stand mixer and knead for 4 minutes or 8 minutes by hand, until the dough is smooth.

2. Divide the dough into 6 parts. Flour each one and roll out with a rolling pin to ¼ inch (⅓ cm) thick or to the number 1 setting on a pasta machine. Flour the sheets of pasta generously. Lay them out flat and cut them into fettuccini-like strips. Or pass them through a fettuccini cutter on a pasta machine. Let the pasta rest for 1 hour.

3. Line up the fettuccini, and with a knife cut the pasta into squares ¼ inch wide (½ cm). At this point you now have crozets! You can let the crozets sit overnight at room temperature (this is ideal) or you can cook them right away. In both cases, cook the pasta in a large pot of salted water for 3 minutes. Drain and serve with olive oil, butter, and a sprinkling of cheese.

Pasta with Arugula-Garlic Persillade and Roquefort

Serves: 2
Preparation time: 10 minutes
Cooking time: 11 to 13 minutes

FOR THE PASTA

Salt for the pasta water
  (see steps)
9 ounces (255 g) quality dried
  pasta (a longer cooking time
  often indicates a good pasta;
  look for pasta with at least 10
  to 11 minutes cooking time)
½ cup (114 ml) cooking water
  from pasta
10 tablespoons (5 ounces;
  142 g) Roquefort or
  blue cheese
4 tablespoons Herbed Bread
  Crumbs (page 27)
Freshly ground black pepper

FOR THE ARUGULA-GARLIC PERSILLADE

4.4 ounces (125 g) arugula, or
  fresh greens or herbs
4 tablespoons olive oil
2 teaspoons minced garlic
½ teaspoon salt

I have always found French cuisine to be on the cautious side with garlic; its use is judicious, lest it mask a more subtle ingredient or leave one with bad breath. One of the more notable exceptions is persillade, a dense green, pesto-like sauce made from parsley and garlic, often used to drench snails. (In my opinion, those who like snails are just in it for the persillade.) The word *persillade* is derivative of *persille,* which means *parsley,* but it also sounds like *persillé,* which means *marbled,* and is reminiscent of the coloring in French cheeses like Roquefort. I had already been making pasta with Roquefort sauce when I discovered that persillade made a wonderful addition, and that it was no coincidence that the two sauces resembled each other in name.

Don't get me wrong, this isn't some over-the-top cream-based sauce. Let the Roquefort melt into the persillade with a little cooking water from the pasta and you'll have a flavorful sauce without the heaviness. The bite of the arugula here keeps the pasta herbaceous and quite light. For extra texture and volume before serving, don't hesitate to pile on some extra arugula leaves and Herbed Bread Crumbs (page 27).

1. Bring a large pot of salted water (about 2 quarts; 2 L) to a boil. As a rule of thumb I usually add 1 teaspoon salt per quart of water. Cook the pasta al dente, or 1 to 2 minutes less than the suggested cooking time. Before draining, reserve ½ cup of the cooking liquid—this is important, so don't forget! Drain the pasta and set it aside.

2. In the meantime, prepare the persillade: Reserve one-quarter of the arugula and place the rest in a food processor or blender. Add the olive oil, garlic, and salt. Blend until combined but still somewhat coarse.

3. In a bowl, use the back of a fork to combine the reserved cooking liquid from the pasta along with the Roquefort. Add the drained pasta back to the pot along with the cheese mixture and the persillade and then stir together over medium-low heat until a smooth and glossy sauce forms, about 1 minute. Divide the pasta between two plates, add the remaining arugula on top, and sprinkle with the bread crumbs and black pepper.

Corsican Chestnut and Ricotta Gnocchi with Za'atar

Serves: 2 to 4
Preparation time: 25 minutes
Cooking time: 9 to 10 minutes
Rest time: 1 hour

1 cup (227 g) ricotta
1 egg yolk
¾ cup (75 g) grated Parmesan
2 teaspoons Za'atar (page 26), plus 1 teaspoon for serving
½ cup (60 g) plus 2 table-spoons chestnut flour or all-purpose or gluten-free flour
½ teaspoon salt
¼ cup (50 g) olive oil
1 cup chard leaves
½ lemon

While ricotta and gnocchi are technically Italian products, they are also what I would consider to be French through marriage. Gnocchi originates from northern Italy, which borders France. The Mediterranean island of Corsica sits comfortably in between the two and incorporates some of the best of French and Italian cuisine into the island's own food culture, hence chestnut gnocchi with Corsican chestnut flour. And while you'll probably want to use ricotta for this recipe, it is similar to Brousse, which is a soft cheese native to Corsica—although one that remains difficult to find outside of France. If you can get your hands on some Brousse, I highly recommend using it here! I also like to add a little Za'atar (page 26) to this gnocchi, because the bright flavors in this spice blend bring a little zing to the rich nuttiness of the chestnut flour. While Za'atar isn't specifically French, the different spices it's made from can almost all be found in France—making it really complementary to French recipes.

1. Stir together the ricotta, egg yolk, and ½ cup of the Parmesan. Add 2 teaspoons of the Za'atar and ½ cup of the chestnut flour. Gently flour a cutting board with the 2 tablespoons chestnut flour. Divide the dough into two parts. Roll one-half of the dough on the cutting board into a cylindrical shape, approximately 8 inches (20 cm) long. Dip your knife in the flour to prevent it from sticking to the dough and cut the gnocchi into ½-inch-long (1 cm) pieces.

2. Bring a large pot of water to a boil and gently scrape the gnocchi directly into the boiling water. If a little flour ends up in the pot as well, it's no big deal. Boil the gnocchi for 2-3 minutes, or until they begin to float up to the surface. Drain and rinse the gnocchi with cold water and gently coat with 1 tablespoon of the olive oil in order to prevent the gnocchi from sticking to each other. Ideally you should allow the gnocchi to rest at room temperature for 1 hour before the next step, but if you're impatient, then just continue ahead.

3. Heat 1 tablespoon of the olive oil in a sauté pan. Add the chard leaves and wilt them for 1 minute, turning frequently. Remove the chard from the pan and divide it between two to four plates.

4. Pan-fry the gnocchi: Add 2 more tablespoons of olive oil to the sauté pan and add the gnocchi. Let the gnocchi lightly brown in the pan, 2 to 3 minutes, before turning them over and cooking for another 2 to 3 minutes. Serve the gnocchi over the chard leaves with a little lemon juice, the remaining ¼ cup grated Parmesan, 1 teaspoon of Za'atar, and sea salt.

Croissant Sandwich with Crispy Mushrooms and Béchamel

Serves: 2
Preparation time: 15 minutes
Cooking time: 18 minutes

FOR THE CRISPY MUSHROOMS

2 cups (174 g) fresh mushrooms
3 tablespoons vegetable
   oil (sunflower, grapeseed,
   or others)
½ teaspoon minced garlic

FOR THE BÉCHAMEL

2 tablespoons butter
1 tablespoon flour
1 cup (227 ml) whole milk
2 tablespoons grated cheese
   (Comté, Cheddar, Swiss,
   Asiago . . .)

TO SERVE

2 croissants
1 handful mesclun greens,
   washed and dried
2 teaspoons thyme, optional
2 tablespoons Mustard Seed
   Caviar (page 34), optional
2 tablespoons mustard (Dijon
   or stone-ground)
Cornichons (page 31) for serving
Pickled Red Onions (page 203)
   for serving

Croissant style sandwiches, once out of fashion in France, have made a recent comeback. Gone are the days of boring ham and melted cheese, because chefs these days use seasonal sautéed vegetables and light garnishes. You will want to use the freshest butter croissants possible. You can also replace the mushrooms with sautéed greens like kale, chard, or asparagus.

1. Clean and dry the mushrooms. Press them between two towels in order to extract the most amount of moisture. Heat the oil in a large frying pan over medium-high heat. Slice the mushrooms thickly, about ¾ inch (2 cm). Panfry them for 5 minutes on the first side. Then turn them over and pan-fry for another 5 minutes on the other side. Stir in the garlic and cook until the mushrooms are slightly crispy, for another 3 to 4 minutes. Leave the mushrooms in the hot pan and set aside, without a lid.

2. Prepare the béchamel. Melt the butter in a small saucepan over medium heat. Whisk in the flour and stir for 30 seconds. Pour in the milk and stir constantly until the sauce thickens, about 3 minutes. Once the sauce is smooth, turn off the heat and whisk in the cheese.

3. To serve: Cut the croissants in half lengthwise. Spoon the béchamel on the inside of the bottom half. Divide the mushrooms between the croissants and place them on top of the béchamel. Add the mesclun greens and thyme, if using, and spoon over the mustard seed caviar. Spread the mustard on the inside of the top half of the croissant. Close the croissant. Serve warm with cornichons and a few of the pickled red onions.

Corsican Chestnut and Ricotta Gnocchi with Za'atar

Croissant Sandwich with Crispy Mushrooms and Béchamel

Croque Madame with Spinach and Béchamel

Serves: 4
Preparation time: 28 minutes
Cooking time: 15 minutes

FOR THE BÉCHAMEL

2 tablespoons butter
1 teaspoon flour
½ cup (114 ml) milk
¼ teaspoon salt

FOR THE CROQUE MADAME

2 tablespoons butter,
   room temperature
4 slices country-style bread
1 cup (113 g) shredded cheese
   (Comté, provolone, white
   Cheddar, Swiss)
2 tablespoons Le Pistou
   (page 34)
2 handfuls of spinach
2 sunny-side up eggs
Freshly ground black pepper

A glorified grilled cheese would be a fair but slightly inaccurate description of a croque madame (with an egg) or croque monsieur (without the egg). Like the classic croque madame, this version has got a cheesy inside and comes dressed with a generous spoon of béchamel sauce, a crispy cheesy crust, and a sunny-side up egg. This is obviously not finger food, so you'll want a fork and knife for this one. I like to add a good handful of spinach, but sliced celery root charcuterie wouldn't be out of place here either. I like to use a mix of different white shredded cheeses, but you can also use just one if you prefer.

1. Preheat the oven to 350°F (180°C) with a sheet pan inside.
2. Prepare the béchamel: Melt the butter in a saucepan. Whisk in the flour, then whisk in the milk. Whisk quickly until the sauce is smooth and thick, about 5 minutes. Stir in the salt and set aside.
3. For the croque madame: Butter one side of each bread slice. Carefully remove the sheet pan from the oven. Turn the bread buttered side down on the sheet pan. Spread the béchamel over these 2 slices of bread, divide ¾ cup of the cheese between the other two slices and place in the oven. Turn the oven on broil and keep an eye as the cheese melts. Just as it begins to brown, about 3 minutes, remove the pan and close the sandwiches. Spread a little pistou on the top of each closed sandwich and sprinkle the last ¼ cup of cheese on top of the sandwiches. Return to the oven until the cheese melts and the sandwich tops begin to turn golden, about 3-4 minutes. Remove from the oven, carefully open the sandwich with a fork, and divide the spinach between each sandwich. It will wilt in a couple minutes time. Serve with an egg on top of each sandwich and a little fresh black pepper.

Spicy Egg Salad Sandwiches on Baguettes

Serves: 4
Preparation time: 15 minutes
Cooking time: 17 minutes

**FOR THE PICKLED
RED ONIONS**

½ cup (114 ml) white or
rice vinegar
½ cup (114 ml) water
1 tablespoon sugar
1 teaspoon salt
1 small red onion, thinly sliced
into rings

FOR THE EGGS

8 eggs
4 tablespoons Mayonnaise
(page 40)
1 tablespoon freshly
grated ginger
1 teaspoon garlic, minced
1 teaspoon Espelette pepper
1 teaspoon salt

TO ASSEMBLE

2 baguettes
¼ English cucumber,
thinly sliced
5 radishes, thinly sliced
2 green onions, thinly sliced
¼ yellow zucchini, thinly sliced
2 tablespoons Mustard Seed
Caviar (page 34)
Espelette pepper to serve

This is a great sandwich for gatherings. Feel free to serve small toasts instead of sandwiches and spread the eggs and vegetables on them. You can make the egg salad as well as the pickled onions the day before, making it a perfect make-ahead picnic sandwich.

1. To make the pickled red onions, heat the white vinegar with the water, sugar, and salt in a small to medium saucepan. Bring to a boil and simmer for 5 minutes. Turn off the heat and add the red onion slices to the pan, making sure they are completely submerged in the brine, and let stand for 1 hour.

2. Meanwhile, bring a medium pot of water to a boil. Carefully add the eggs to the pot with a skimmer. Remove 2 eggs after 8 minutes, and put aside. The soft-cooked yolks are pretty and adds texture to the sandwich. Cook the rest of the eggs for a total of 12 minutes. Immediately after cooking, quickly rinse the eggs under cold water and let them cool to room temperature. Peel and quarter the softer-cooked eggs lengthwise. Peel and chop the rest of the eggs and mix with the mayonnaise, ginger, garlic, Espelette pepper, and salt. Place in the refrigerator for 1 hour or up to 1 day before assembling the sandwiches.

3. Cut the baguettes crosswise into sandwich-sized lengths, then cut them in half lengthwise. Fill the baguettes with the egg salad, place the vegetables on top, and garnish with the 8-minute egg quarters, pickled red onions, and mustard seed caviar. Serve with a little extra Espelette pepper.

Buckwheat Galette with Asparagus

Serves: 4
Preparation time: 15 minutes
Cooking time: 40 minutes
Rest time: 2 hours

2 cups (480 g) buckwheat flour
5 eggs
4⅓ cups (454 ml) water
1 tablespoon salt
Olive oil for the pan
12 green asparagus stalks
1 tablespoon butter
1 cup (113 g) grated
  cheese (Cheddar, Swiss,
  Gouda, or a mix)
Sea salt to taste

You may know this dish better as a crêpe, but technically, when it's savory, it's considered a galette. This classic buckwheat batter is often made in large quantities. If you want to make less, you could cut the recipe in half, but then you would have to split the amount of egg in half. I say just make it all and use the leftovers to make Buckwheat Chips (page 67).

A crêpe pan is ideal for making crêpes and galettes. I didn't believe it and figured that a normal sautée pan (with sides obviously) could do the job just fine. And it did for a while. But then came the day I got myself a crêpe pan. Now I swear by it. For this recipe, you'll want to have your longest flipper spatula at the ready, perhaps even two, and a bottle of hard cider in the fridge because the latter is undeniably the drink of choice when eating galettes.

1. Prepare the buckwheat batter: Pour the buckwheat flour into a large bowl. Make a hole in the middle and crack 1 of the eggs inside. Add the water and salt and quickly whisk together until you have a smooth and slightly thick batter. Let your batter sit for 2 hours at room temperature. Alternatively, you can prepare the batter in advance and leave it in the fridge overnight.

2. Heat a crêpe pan or a large sauté pan over medium-low heat. Pour in a small amount of oil and coat the entire pan with the help of either a pastry brush or a piece of paper towel. Pour in enough batter to completely, yet thinly, cover the pan, spreading out to the edges with your spatula. Cook until it is covered in small bubbles, 1 to 2 minutes. Flip over gently with the spatula, and cook on the other side for 30 seconds. Slide the galette off of the pan and onto a large plate. The galette will cool down, but no worries. Repeat this process until you have used all the batter and you have four galettes. Set the galettes aside.

3. Prepare the asparagus: Break off the bottom ends of the asparagus and discard. Place a steamer basket inside a deep pot with a fitted lid. Fill the pot with boiling water up to the bottom of the steam basket. Steam the asparagus for 3 to 5 minutes depending on their thickness. Remove the asparagus from the steamer and cut each stalk crosswise into two or three pieces and set aside.

4. Once you are ready to assemble your galettes, heat up your pan and lightly brush it with the butter. Place a galette on the pan. Sprinkle the center of the galette generously with cheese. Make a little hole in the cheese and break an egg inside. Delicately spread the egg white away from the center and on to the cheese, this will help the egg cook more evenly—especially if you want to serve the yolk whole. If you prefer to serve the yolk cooked, then this is the point at which you should break it and spread it over the cheese as well. Continue to cook until the egg whites are just about set, approximately 6 minutes. Place some of the asparagus on top of the egg and cheese and fold in the sides of the galette to make a sort of crust-like border, then slide the galette out of the pan and directly onto a plate. Continue cooking the last three galettes in this manner. If you'd like to keep them warm as you cook, place the plates as you go along in a warm oven, approximately 140°F (60°C).

5. Sprinkle sea salt on the galettes just before serving and enjoy.

Open-Faced Cheese and Herb Omelette

Serves: 1
Preparation time: 5 minutes
Cooking time: 3 minutes

2 medium organic eggs
(see Note)

Pinch of sea salt, plus more
for serving

1.7 ounces (48 g) dry cheese
(Parmesan or Cheddar), aged
6 months or more (fresher
cheeses like goat cheese or
feta are nice too)

1½ teaspoons butter

1 teaspoon olive oil

2 tablespoons fresh
herbs, minced

1 tablespoon scallion,
rinsed and dried

Freshly ground black pepper

Maybe you are intimidated by omelettes. But once you know how to make this one, you'll gain confidence. This omelette is light and delicate. My secret is to forget the whole folding part and serve it open faced, therefore almost making it impossible to overcook or scorch the eggs. I use a small, cast-iron skillet or nonstick pan just hot enough to make the butter frothy, and I always have my eggs already whisked and at the ready. From that point on it's just a couple minutes until this omelette is on the plate. All that is left to do is finely, yet generously, grate some aged cheese on top (finely grated cheese as an open-faced topping won't turn tough and chewy, as often happens in a folded omelette), and then sprinkle on some fresh herbs. If you do want to make a classic folded omelette, I suggest you make this open faced a couple times. Once you've got the tucking part down, move on up to the folded version, using the side of the pan to fold the omelette over itself.

1. Whisk the eggs and a pinch of salt together, until combined, approximately 30 seconds. Set aside. Have the cheese nearby, along with a cheese grater that grates on a small grade. If you are using packaged grated cheese, choose the smallest grade possible.

2. Heat the butter and olive oil in a small cast-iron skillet or nonstick pan over medium heat. Once it starts to bubble, add half the herbs. Cook the frothy butter mixture for 1 minute. Spread the herbs evenly around the skillet or pan. Have a spatula ready. Pour in the whisked egg. It should sizzle immediately. Be prepared to turn off the heat in 30 seconds. Shake the pan a little and then use your spatula to gently push the sides of the egg slightly toward the center to keep the omelette in a neat circle. The omelette should be 6 to 8 inches (15 to 20 cm) in diameter.

3. After 30 seconds, turn off the heat and move the pan off the hot burner. Use the spatula to spread the uncooked egg away from the center and to the sides of the pan, tilting the pan when necessary and each time tucking them back into the omelette once they cook. It shouldn't cook long, this is a 2-minute affair tops. You don't want an overcooked omelette, so leave some of the egg runny, as it will continue to cook even when you slide it out of the pan. At this point, you can decide to slide the omelette onto a plate or just eat it straight from the skillet or pan. Grate the cheese all over the omelette. It should look like fresh snow. Sprinkle with the rest of the fresh herbs, sea salt, and fresh black pepper. Serve immediately.

NOTE: If your pan is larger than 9 inches (23 cm) in diameter, you might want to make a 3-egg omelette instead of a 2-egg omelette, in order to avoid overcooking. But don't attempt to make 4- or 5-egg omelettes with this technique.

In France, omelettes are most often served *baveuse,* which means just slightly runny inside. If you like yours cooked through, then plan on removing the omelette from the heat at the 30-second mark, but leave it in the pan for another 3 minutes so that it will continue to cook through.

Stuffed Cabbage Leaves with Mushrooms and Lentil-Walnut Rice Pilaf

Serves: 2
Preparation time: 20 minutes
Cooking time: 1 hour
15 minutes

¾ cup (139 g) whole-grain rice
3 cups (681 ml) water
¾ cup (149 g) lentils
¼ cup (60 ml) white wine
½ teaspoon minced garlic
1 tablespoon fresh rosemary or
   1 teaspoon dried
1 tablespoon walnut oil
2 tablespoons chopped walnuts
1 tablespoon fresh thyme or
   1 teaspoon dried
1 teaspoon salt
1 tablespoon olive oil
2 cups (156 g) ½-inch (1 cm)
   diced mushrooms (white,
   shiitake, or other)
6 large cabbage leaves
2 tablespoons Dijon or stone-
   ground mustard, optional

Easy to wrap and particularly hearty, I first made these when I had some leftover rice pilaf in the fridge. I'd suggest you also take that approach too. While I particularly like to use mushrooms when making any sort of stuffing, you can also substitute other seasonal vegetables in place of them.

1. In a large pot, bring the rice and water to a boil, lower the heat, and simmer for 20 minutes. Add the lentils, white wine, minced garlic, rosemary, walnut oil, walnuts, half of the thyme sprigs and salt and cook over low heat for another 20 minutes.
2. Heat the olive oil in a large nonstick frying pan. Add the mushrooms and sauté for 10 minutes, or until they are no longer humid and almost crispy. Stir the mushrooms into the rice and let the mixture cool.
3. Bring another large pot of water to a boil. Boil the cabbage leaves 3 at a time for 5 minutes each batch until they are supple. Remove and place on a towel to dry. Once the cabbage and the filling have cooled to the touch, begin stuffing the cabbage.
4. Place 2 tablespoons of the rice filling in the bottom half of a cabbage leaf. Fold the sides in and then roll the leaf away from you, keeping the sides tucked in as you do so. Place a skewer or a couple toothpicks through the sides of the stuffed cabbage to keep it intact. Continue this process with the rest of the cabbage leaves. Place the stuffed cabbage leaves in a steamer basket. Steam for 15 minutes, or until the leaves are tender. Remove the skewers or toothpicks before serving. Serve warm with a little Dijon mustard.

Open-Faced Cheese and Herb Omelette

BOHÈME COOKING

Stuffed Cabbage Leaves with Mushrooms and Lentil-Walnut Rice Pilaf

BOHÈME COOKING

Salad Quiche with Feta and Pickled Red Onions

Serves: 4
Preparation time: 25 minutes
Cooking time: 45 minutes

1 teaspoon butter
1 puff pastry
5 medium organic eggs
1 cup (227 g) crème fraîche or
    sour cream
8 ounces (228 g) crumbled feta
1 teaspoon salt
1 cup roughly chopped herbs
¼ cup (40 g) minced red onion
Pickled Red Onions
    (page 203), optional

Sometimes quiche can overpromise—too many flavors, ingredients, vegetables, and cheese. To be honest, I felt burned out on quiche after a few years of living in Paris. But that all changed when I first saw a salad style quiche in Marseille. I was there as a guest chef at Provisions, a bookstore turned grocer and restaurant owned by two local women. It's open only three days a week, and in their spare time the two owners spend their time seeking out local farmers and wildflowers, hiking with natural wine producers, and picnicking year-round on the jagged coast. I had been invited by the owners to cook for the weekend in order to promote my latest book. While there, I noted their *systeme D* scrappy chic, DYI approach to work and life. I also noticed their quiche. It was simple, low on filling, and piled high with feta, herbs, and red onions. It was un-quiche-like, with uncharacteristic freshness and tanginess—exactly what I needed in order to become enthralled with quiche again.

1. Preheat the oven to 350°F (180°C). Lightly butter a 10- to 12-inch (25 to 30 cm) quiche or pie pan. Place the puff pastry in the pie pan and press down around the crust to help it hold on to the edges of the pan—no need for any type of ornate crust though. Poke the bottom of the pastry all over with a fork. Whisk together the eggs, crème fraîche, half the feta, and the salt. Pour the egg mixture into the quiche or pie pan. Place in the oven and bake until the center is no longer liquid and the edges are golden, about 45 minutes.

2. Remove from the oven and let the quiche cool until warm or room temperature or even cold—the choice is yours. Sprinkle with the chopped herbs, pickled red onions, and the rest of the feta. You can also make this quiche the day before and reheat or serve it cold.

NOTE: In France, quiche is simple fare and shouldn't be time consuming. Here, both home cooks and, somewhat surprisingly, professionals use premade feuilleté quiche crust. Personally, I think that puff pastry does a pretty fine job. If you want to make your own crust, I'd suggest something simple that is in the spirit of quiche and comes together quickly, like the crust from the Rustic Carrot Tarte with Burrata and Fennel Dukkah (page 179). If you want to make feuilletté, you can follow the recipe for the dough in the Flute Crackers with Herbes de Provence and Seeds (page 70).

Ratatouille with Rustic Croutons and Poached Eggs

Serves: 4
Preparation time: 15 minutes
Cooking time: 1 hour 38 minutes

FOR THE RATATOUILLE

2 tablespoons olive oil
1 medium onion (white or yellow), thinly sliced
½ teaspoon minced garlic
½ pound (227 g) eggplant
½ pound (227 g) tomatoes
½ pound (227 g) zucchini
⅓ pound (150 g) bell pepper (red, green, or other color)
1 tablespoon fresh thyme
½ teaspoon Espelette pepper or other light chili powder, plus more for serving
1 teaspoon salt
Croutons (page 27) for serving

FOR THE POACHED EGGS

½ cup (114 ml) white vinegar
2½ cups (568 ml) water
4 eggs
4 thyme sprigs for serving

Some people prepare their ratatouille vegetables in small diced cubes, or in slices laid out in a pan. But those methods were always a little too fussy for me. I learned the secrets to making a rustic ratatouille just after I moved to France. I was often cooking ratatouille for the family for whom I was working as an au pair, and they didn't hold back on giving me pointers. These are the two lessons I learned: First, don't overdo it on the garlic (as a young American who had just arrived in Paris, I had the tendency to do this . . .) because you don't mask the flavor of the vegetables and herbs. And second, cook the vegetables until they melt together and have a jammy texture, meaning that even if you think it's done cooking, it probably isn't. Taste it, and if there is any resistance, then put it back on the stove. A few years after leaving my au pair job, my ex-husband showed me how to serve this as a meal in itself with poached eggs and croutons, and I've never looked back!

1. Heat the olive oil in a large pot (preferably cast iron) over medium-low heat. Add the onion and garlic to the pot and cook, stirring frequently until the onions become translucent, about 5 minutes. If the edges of the onions start to brown, turn down the heat. Wash and chop the rest of the vegetables into 1½- to 2-inch (4 to 5 cm) pieces. They should be rather large as they will cook down to half their size. Add them to the pot along with the thyme, Espelette pepper, and salt. Lower the heat and cook for 30 minutes. The vegetables might look a little dry, but don't be tempted to add more water or oil, they will loosen up as they continue to cook. Place a lid on the pot and cook for at least another hour, stirring every 10 minutes. The vegetables will melt together, more or less, but stir carefully so as not to completely smash them.

2. To make the poached eggs, heat the vinegar and water in a small-medium saucepan. Once the water is boiling, crack in the eggs quickly, one after the next. Cook the eggs for 3 minutes without disturbing them. Prepare a medium salad bowl filled with cold water. Remove the eggs from the water carefully with a skimmer and place them in the cold water bath. Drain once and fill again with cold water. The cold water will keep them from overcooking, but as the water turns warm from the eggs' heat, it will keep the eggs just the right temperature for serving.

3. To serve, divide the ratatouille between four shallow bowls. Place a poached egg on top and sprinkle with croutons, more Espelette pepper if you like, and a sprig of fresh thyme.

DESSERTS

6

Many people find French desserts intimidating, and I used to be one of them. Not only did I see little leeway in the recipes, I felt like I would never have the right equipment or ingredients that were called for. Plus, having finally moved to a country where it was normal to eat glorious, unpasteurized cheese after the main course, I couldn't get enough of it and so I rarely had room for an extra treat.

The novelty of cheese still hasn't worn off, but dessert and I get along much better these days—having kids and entertaining on a weekly basis will do that. Now when I have friends over for what I know will be a dessert evening, because there are those evenings that just simply aren't, I don't avoid it. In fact, I'm even happy to make a dessert and bring it to a friend's place. What made the big difference for me was learning a few tricks, such as turning old croissants into a showstopper brunch dessert (page 234), a beaten egg into a souffléed crêpe (page 230), or a cheater's mille-feuille layered with squares of filo dough (page 220). Now I'm no longer looking for a way out of dessert.

And if you happen to be someone who finds French desserts intimidating, worrying you don't have the right equipment or ingredients, these recipes are for you *ma chère.* Most of them don't require anything fancy and come together in less than an hour. And if you're missing something like almond flour, then I'll give you a trick for grinding it up yourself.

Grape and Thyme Tarte with Whipped Labneh

Serves: 6
Preparation time: 20 minutes
Cooking time: 23 minutes

FOR THE CRUST
⅓ cup (75 g) butter
½ cup (168 g) honey
2 cups (178 g) oats
1 cup (80 g) packed
   almond slivers
⅔ cup (64 g) almond flour
   (see Note)

FOR THE FILLING
⅔ cup (151 ml) heavy cream
½ cup (114 g) cream cheese
½ cup (114 g) Marinated
   Labneh Balls (page 48) or
   store-bought, or mascarpone
   or ricotta
¼ cup (50 g) granulated sugar
1 pound grapes (454 g)
1 tablespoon fresh thyme leaves

When autumn comes, I am always missing the fruit tartes of summer. This one is a great mid-season compromise. You can substitute mascarpone or ricotta for the labneh if you prefer. If you can't find almond flour, just toss some toasted almonds (blanched or not) in your food processor or blender, and mix on high speed for one minute. And if you don't have either one of those tools, wrapping up the almonds in a towel and giving the bundle a few whacks with a rolling pin will do the trick.

1. Preheat the oven to 325°F (160°C) and lightly oil an 8-by-10-inch (20-by-25 cm) tarte pan.
2. Prepare the crust: Melt the butter and honey together in a saucepan until it begins to lightly simmer. Remove from the heat. Add the oats, almond slivers, and almond flour and stir well. Place your tarte pan on top of a sheet pan for extra stability. Pour the oat mixture into the tarte pan and let it cool for 5 minutes, or until it's just warm to the touch. Press the oat mixture into the sides and the bottom of the tarte pan so that it forms a crust. Place the tarte crust in the oven on the sheet pan and bake for 20 to 22 minutes, until golden. Remove and let cool completely.
3. Prepare the whipped labneh: In a large bowl, beat the heavy cream for 2 minutes with a stand or hand mixer on low speed. Slowly increase the speed to medium and allow the cream to thicken. Add the cream cheese and labneh, spoon by spoon, beating in between additions. Beat on a higher speed until the mixture begins to thicken even more. Then add the sugar and beat on the fastest speed until you have a whipped cream. Add the whipped labneh cream to the cooled tarte crust and use a spatula to spread it evenly and smooth out the surface. Cut the grapes in half and place on the tarte cut side facing up. Sprinkle with the fresh thyme. Serve immediately or refrigerate and serve the same day.

NOTE: If you are making your own almond flour, I'd suggest toasting the almonds first in an oven at 320°F (160°C) for 8 minutes. Let the toasted almonds cool before grinding them down into a flour.

Easy Orange Custard Mille-Feuille with Kumquats

Serves: 2 to 4
Preparation time: 30 minutes
Rest time: 2 hours
Cooking time: 18 minutes

FOR THE CUSTARD
4 egg yolks
4 tablespoons sugar
2 tablespoons flour
3 cups (681 ml) whole milk

FOR THE PASTRY
10 sheets filo pastry
5 tablespoons melted butter
4 tablespoons powdered sugar
10 kumquats
1 orange for zesting

While not technically a legit mille-feuille, and requiring much less work than the traditional pastry of a thousand layers calls for, this dish still makes for a show-off dessert. The filo dough gives a wonderfully crispy sensation as you break through to creamy custard. This cheat version of mille-feuille can be thrown together quickly, and both components can be made in advance and plated just before you serve.

1. To make the custard, whisk together the egg yolks with the sugar and flour in a large, heat-resistant bowl. Meanwhile, bring the milk to a boil in a medium saucepan. Slowly pour the steaming milk in a thin stream into the egg and sugar mixture, whisking constantly, about 4 minutes. Pour the mixture back into the saucepan and bring to a simmer, again whisking constantly until the custard thickens, about 5 minutes. Pour the custard into a clean bowl, let cool, and then refrigerate for 2 hours.

2. To make the pastry, preheat the oven to 350°F (180°F) and lightly oil three baking sheets. Brush the filo pastry sheets lightly with the melted butter and cut the pastry into 3-by-4-inch (8-by-10 cm) rectangles (or a similar form) and place the rectangles on your prepared baking sheets. Using a sieve, sprinkle the pastry rectangles with 2 tablespoons of the powdered sugar. Bake the filo for 6 to 8 minutes, until golden. Let cool. Sprinkle with another 2 tablespoons of the powdered sugar.

3. Slice the kumquats thinly. Heat a small frying pan over medium-low heat and place the kumquat slices flat in the pan. Sprinkle with the remaining 1 tablespoon powdered sugar and caramelize for 1 minute. Remove the kumquats from the pan and let them cool.

4. To serve, place a rectangular sheet of filo on a plate. Spread a tablespoon of custard over the filo, without spreading to the edges. Place another sheet of filo on top and repeat the process until you have 3 layers of custard and 4 layers of filo. Continue with the other plates. Grate orange zest on top using a microplane or a four-sided box grater. Sprinkle with the candied kumquats and serve right away.

Poached Rhubarb with Whipped Mascarpone

Serves: 4
Preparation time: 5 minutes
Cooking time: 5 to 10 minutes

FOR THE POACHED RHUBARB
¾ cup (171 ml) rice vinegar
1⅔ cup (303 ml) water
½ (99 g) sugar
3 rhubarb stalks, sliced into
  2-inch (5 cm) pieces

**FOR THE WHIPPED
MASCARPONE**
⅔ cup (151 ml) heavy whipping
  cream, chilled
⅔ cup (151 g) mascarpone
½ cup (99 g) sugar

Fresh basil leaves, optional
Freshly ground Szechuan
  peppercorns, optional

I like to poach rhubarb in a light syrup with a good splash of rice vinegar to retain tanginess. This makes for a simple spring dessert that's spooned over whipped mascarpone, and also leaves you with the syrupy beginnings of a delicious cocktail.

1. To make the poached rhubarb: In a small saucepan, bring the rice vinegar, water, and sugar to a boil. Add the rhubarb pieces and reduce the heat to barely a simmer for 2 minutes. Turn off the heat and let the rhubarb sit for another 2 to 5 minutes, until you can gently slide a knife into a stalk with little effort. Thinner rhubarb will poach quicker than the thicker stalks. Using a skimmer, remove the rhubarb from the syrup and let the pieces and syrup cool. If you'd like, reduce the remaining syrup for another 5 to 10 minutes for a more concentrated flavor.

2. For the whipped mascarpone: Pour the heavy cream into the bowl of a stand mixer and whip with the whisk attachment on low for 3 minutes. If you don't have a stand mixer, you can also whip by hand with a whisk, ideally in a chilled metal bowl. Add the mascarpone and continue to whip. Once the mixture begins to thicken, add the sugar. Continue to whip until it holds form, and be careful not to over-whip or it will turn into butter.

3. Divide the whipped mascarpone among four bowls, place the poached rhubarb on top along with the basil leaves. Drizzle with a couple spoons of rhubarb syrup and a crack of Szechuan peppercorn on top (great for its tangy grapefruit flavor). Serve right away!

Honey Lemon Madeleines

Makes: 12 to 14 madeleines
Preparation time: 5 minutes
Cooking time: 16 minutes

½ cup (113 g) melted butter

½ cup (99 g) sugar

½ cup (105 g) plus 1 tablespoon egg whites (about
  3 large eggs)

½ cup (60 g) flour

½ cup (48 g) almond powder

1 teaspoon lemon juice

1 teaspoon lemon zest

1 teaspoon honey

1 tablespoon bee
  pollen, optional

I had written off madeleines before even really trying them. They seemed to me an overly bourgeoise and complicated way of making what was more or less a simple cake. I had also come to associate them with summer tourists flooding the Normand coast and taking home boxes filled with prepackaged industrial versions. But madeleines have a special place in the heart of French food culture, thanks to writer Marcel Proust. His love for madeleines (and the Normand coast) as a boy coined one of the country's favorite food expressions, *"la madeleine de Proust,"* which is a way of describing one's fondest childhood culinary memory. I had figured that madeleines would be difficult to bake, but it turned out to be a piece of cake—which, in case you're wondering, is not a French culinary expression. Although the classic madeleine mold is a gorgeous silver piece, it turns out that silicone molds are what most French bakers, and now I myself, use. But if you don't have a madeleine mold, don't worry. You can cheat a little and bake them in a baking dish or other mold.

1. Whisk the melted butter together with the sugar in a medium bowl. Add the egg whites and whisk until combined. In a separate bowl whisk the flour and almond powder together and then pour the dry mixture into the bowl with the wet ingredients. Stir to combine and then add the lemon juice, lemon zest, and honey. Refrigerate the batter for at least 4 hours.

2. Preheat the oven to 350°F (180°C). Gently oil a madeleine mold or either a small 10-inch (25 cm) square baking dish or a silicone 10-piece cupcake mold. Pour the batter among the molds or in the baking dish. Sprinkle with pollen if using. Bake for 14 to 16 minutes until golden brown. Allow the madeleines to cool before removing from the molds or baking dish. If using the baking dish, cut the madeleines into squares before using. Serve any time of the day, with breakfast, afternoon coffee, or as a light dessert.

Honey Lemon Madeleines

Blueberry Yogurt Cake

Serves: 4 to 6
Preparation time: 15 minutes
Cooking time: 45 minutes

⅓ cup (66 ml) vegetable
   oil, plus 1 tablespoon for
   greasing the pan
5 eggs
1¾ cup (347 g) sugar
¾ cup (170 g) yogurt
2/3 cup (132 ml) vegetable oil
3 cups (360 g) plus
   1 tablespoon flour
16 g baking powder
1½ cups blueberries
2 tablespoons powdered
   sugar, optional

Gâteau au yaourt, or yogurt cake, is one of the most requested desserts among French children. Luckily, its simplicity means that many adults know the recipe by heart and can teach it to their children. Traditionally, everything in this recipe is measured with yogurt containers (one of the few times I know the French to measure with anything but the metric system). The yogurt makes this batter creamy, and because of it you need to use less oil. And, of course, you can substitute other berries, pears, or summer stone fruits in place of blueberries.

1. Preheat the oven to 350°F (180°C). Lightly grease a 10-inch (25 cm) springform pan or a loaf pan with the tablespoon of vegetable oil.

2. Whisk the eggs and sugar together in either a stand mixer or in a large bowl with a whisk until the mixture is very frothy. Stir in the yogurt and vegetable oil. In a separate bowl, whisk together the 3 cups of flour and the baking powder. Add the dry ingredients to the wet and stir until combined.

3. Pour the batter into the pan. In a small bowl, toss the blueberries with the last tablespoon of flour. This will prevent them from sinking to the bottom of the cake. Add half the blueberries to the batter in the pan and stir gently so that they spread out through the cake. Sprinkle the rest of the blueberries on top of the batter. Place the cake in the oven and bake for 40 to 45 minutes, until the top of the cake is golden brown, slightly puffy, and a knife comes out clean when inserted into the center. Let the cake cool completely and sprinkle with powdered sugar to serve.

Cherry Clafoutis with Toasted Almonds

Serves: 4 to 6
Preparation time: 20 minutes
Cooking time: 40 minutes

1 pound (454 g) fresh cherries, washed and pitted (see Note)
1 tablespoon butter
2 eggs plus 2 egg yolks
¾ cup (149 g) sugar
1¾ cups (397 ml) whole milk
½ cup (48 g) almond flour or regular white flour
½ cup (28 g) cornstarch
¼ cup (20 g) almond slivers

This recipe is inspired by my friend Julie. We met in 2020 when France was in its strictest phase of Covid confinement. I know, kind of an odd moment to make new friends. I was staying on the Normand coast with my boyfriend, my kids, and their father—in separate apartments of course—and we were all going stir-crazy. The sleepy seaside building was almost empty aside from another family who we didn't know, but seeing as they had two boys the same age as my daughters, we got to know each other fairly quickly. None of us were really seeing other families, and once we assessed the risk—kind of like when you decide to date someone exclusively—we decided to make the best of it and confine our families together. Dinner parties and birthdays followed over the course of two months. This clafoutis is inspired by one of the recipes Julie made for us—the cherries had come early that year, but she also admitted to me that frozen cherries would work just fine too.

1. Preheat oven to 350°F (180°C). Leave the cherries whole as much as possible. Butter an 8-by-10-inch (20-by-25 cm) baking dish and spread the cherries out in the dish. Set this aside.
2. In a large bowl, whisk together the eggs, egg yolks, and sugar. Then incorporate the milk little by little. Add the almond flour and cornstarch and whisk until the batter is smooth. Pour the batter over the cherries and sprinkle the top of the batter with the slivered almonds. Bake until slightly puffy and golden, 35 to 40 minutes. Allow the clafoutis to cool and serve either warm or cold.

NOTE: If using frozen cherries, let them thaw completely and press out excess juice with a colander before using.

Souffléed Crêpes with Summer Fruit

Serves: 4 to 6, and makes about 4 to 6 additional crêpes (without filling)
Preparation time: 10 minutes
Cooking time: 11 to 13 minutes

This recipe is almost better with day-old crêpes, so go ahead and have your crêpes—then eat the extras soufflé style. The soufflé filling may sound intimidating, but really it's not. You just need an electric beater or a stand mixer to get the job done. If you make the crêpes ahead of time, it only takes 5 minutes to whip up the soufflé filling and then put everything in the oven. If you're looking for an impressive brunch dessert, this is it.

FOR THE CRÊPES

2 cups (454 ml) milk
¼ cup (50 g) granulated sugar
2 eggs
1 tablespoon butter, melted
1¾ cups (225 g) plus
   1 tablespoon flour
1 teaspoon vegetable oil

FOR THE SOUFFLÉ FILLING

4 eggs
¼ cup (50 g) plus
   1 tablespoon sugar
¼ cup (30 g) flour
2 tablespoons orange juice
¼ teaspoon salt
¼ cup (85 g) jam (berry, peach, apricot)

FOR THE SUMMER FRUIT

2 tablespoons powdered sugar
1 cup (140 g) fresh summer fruit (berries, peaches, apricots), sliced
Maple syrup for serving

1. To make the crêpes, warm the milk in a medium saucepan over low heat until it is warm to the touch, but not hot. Pour it into a mixing bowl and whisk in the granulated sugar, eggs, and melted butter. Add the flour and whisk again until smooth. If there are lumps in the batter, don't hesitate to use a blender for 30 seconds to smooth anything out. Place the batter in the refrigerator for at least 1 hour or up to 1 night.

2. Heat an 11-inch (28 cm) nonstick crêpe pan or a medium frying pan over medium-low heat. Lightly oil the pan with the vegetable oil and a pastry brush or paper towel. Pour about ⅓ cup batter into the pan and immediately tilt the pan and use a spoon to spread the batter evenly to the edges of the pan. Cook the crêpe for 1 minute and then, using a large spatula, flip to the other side. Continue to cook for another 30 seconds on the other side. Place the finished crêpe on a plate and continue this process until all the batter is gone. As you go, cover the plate with a towel or aluminum foil to keep the crêpes warm.

3. Preheat the oven to 350°F (180°C) and prepare a baking sheet either lined with parchment paper or lightly buttered.

4. Prepare the soufflé filling: Separate the egg whites from the yolks. In a medium bowl, whisk together the yolks with ¼ cup of the sugar, flour, and orange juice. In another bowl, beat the egg whites with the salt until they come together and begin to fluff up. Add the remaining tablespoon of granulated sugar to the egg whites and beat at high speed until the whites are fairly stiff and fluffy. Add the egg yolk mixture to the egg white mixture and gently stir together with a spatula until combined.

5. Place two crêpes on a baking sheet. Scoop out one-quarter of the soufflé filling and spread this across half of each crêpe. Fold the crêpe shut and sprinkle with some of the powdered sugar. Repeat with the two remaining crêpes on a second baking sheet. Bake the soufflé crêpes until they are lightly golden, 8 to 10 minutes. Remove from the oven, spoon the fruit on top, drizzle with a little maple syrup, and serve immediately—because soufflé waits for no one!

My Daughters' Vegan Crêpes

Serves: 4
Preparation time: 5 minutes
Cooking time: 15 minutes

1 cup (120 g) flour

2 tablespoon sugar

1 cup (227 ml) plus 1 tablespoon almond milk

2 tablespoons vegetable oil (grapeseed, safflower, sunflower), plus 1 teaspoon for the crêpe pan

½ teaspoon almond extract, optional

Breakfast in bed is a weekend tradition for us, and my daughters recently decided that they were old enough to return the favor. We happened to be out of eggs that particular morning, but they were really set on making crêpes.

In the end I found this recipe to be less heavy than traditional egg-based crêpes, and now it's become my go-to recipe. The lightness is a good thing, especially if you cover your crêpe with chocolate hazelnut spread, as we often do. Even though maple syrup isn't native to France, it obviously does go well over crêpes. But if you want to try something new and more French, try spooning jam inside your crêpes, sprinkle with a little sugar and lemon juice, or make the recipe for Chocolate Hazelnut Spread (page 239) and use that.

1. Place all the ingredients in a blender and blend for 30 seconds. Alternatively, if you don't have a blender on hand, you can whisk together the flour and sugar and then the almond milk, vegetable oil, and almond extract, if using. Whisk the batter until smooth. Let the batter rest, ideally for 30 minutes or overnight. If you're impatient or pressed for time, the crêpes will still come out all right if made immediately.

2. Heat an 11-inch (28 cm) nonstick crêpe pan over medium-low heat. Lightly oil the pan with the teaspoon of vegetable oil and a pastry brush or paper towel. Pour about ⅓ to ½ cup batter onto the pan. Immediately tilt the pan and use a spoon to spread the batter evenly to the edges of the pan. Cook for 2 minutes and then, using a large spatula, flip to the other side. Continue to cook for another 30 seconds on the other side. Serve immediately or prepare all the crêpes one after the next and reheat them individually in the pan over low heat or warm in the oven at 320°F (160°C) for 2 minutes just before serving.

3. Leftover crêpes reheat well after a couple days as long as they are covered.

BOHÈME COOKING

Almond-Buckwheat Croissants

Serves: 4
Preparation time: 10 minutes
Cooking time: 16 minutes

½ cup (114 ml) water
⅔ cup (132 g) sugar
¼ cup (57 g) melted butter
⅔ cup (56 g) almond powder
¼ teaspoon almond extract
1 egg
4 croissants
2 tablespoons almond slivers
2 tablespoons buckwheat
  groats, optional
1 tablespoon powdered sugar

This recipe lets you in on a little secret. What do boulangeries do with leftover croissants? And what can you do with your dried-out croissant? It took me an embarrassingly long amount of time until I realized that my favorite almond croissants were actually old croissants repurposed by the boulangerie. But now that I know, I like to make them myself, testing out different ingredients like buckwheat, strawberry jam, or chocolate.

1. Preheat the oven to 350°F (180°C) and prepare a lightly oiled baking sheet.
2. Heat the water and ⅓ cup of the sugar in a small saucepan over medium-low heat for about 4 minutes. Once it boils, turn off the heat and set aside to cool. In a medium bowl, stir together the melted butter with the remaining ⅓ cup of sugar, almond powder, and almond extract. Add the egg and stir until the mixture is smooth, creating an almond paste.
3. Cut open the croissants lengthwise and place them on the baking sheet. Pour the sugar water into a shallow bowl and dip the croissants into the sugar water, inside and out. Spread 1 tablespoon of almond paste inside each of the croissants. Close the croissants. Spoon the rest of the almond paste on top of the croissants and sprinkle with the almond slivers, buckwheat (if using), and powdered sugar. Bake the croissants for 10 to 12 minutes, until the edges are slightly brown and crispy. Let the croissants cool down for 10 minutes and then serve.

NOTE: You can easily turn these into chocolate-almond croissants or even raspberry-almond croissants by adding a few chocolate squares or spoons of jam to the inside of the croissant.

Chocolate Rosemary Macarons

Makes: 24 macarons
Preparation time: 1 hour
Rest time: Overnight
Cooking time: 16 minutes

FOR THE MACARON SHELLS

1⅓ cups (128g) almond powder
1⅓ cups (150g)
   confectioner's sugar
¼ cup (21g) unsweetened
   Dutch-process cocoa powder
3 egg whites (100 g)
¾ cup + 5 teaspoons sugar
   (143 g + 21 g)
¼ cup (50 ml) water

FOR THE GANACHE FILLING

9 ounces (255 g) dark baking
   chocolate chunks
½ cup (125 ml) whole milk
2 sprigs fresh rosemary,
   for topping

I had long stayed away from certain types of French pastry, specifically anything involving thermometers and slow stirring over double boilers. I also wasn't very interested in recipes that had become omnipresent in almost any international airport terminal (as macarons have). But when I was asked to teach a class on them, I figured it was time to get past my macaron fear. My kids were also game for a long weekend of recipe testing before the actual class.

In the end, these light almond confections didn't require a pastry degree, nor did they need any food coloring. After a first bake I quickly got the piping down—just as you will too. I love the herbaceous note of rosemary in this recipe (and once the holidays come around, a rosemary sprig makes for a festive Christmas decoration). But feel free to change up the topping. You can do away with it completely or add lavender or almond slivers in place of the rosemary.

NOTE: I would strongly recommend making this recipe using the metric measurements along with a scale. The other desserts in this chapter are forgiving in terms of weighing and measuring, but macarons—a little less so. But you don't have to equip yourself with a thermometer for this recipe, nor do you have to have pastry tips, feel free to use them, but a careful eye and a ziplock bag will also do the trick.

1. Sift the almond powder, confectioner's sugar, and unsweetened cocoa powder into the same bowl. Whisk to combine.

2. Prepare an Italian style meringue: Begin whipping half of the egg whites in the bowl of a stand mixer using the whisk attachment. Whip on low speed until the mixture starts to become frothy white, add 1 teaspoon of sugar and whip for 2 to 3 minutes. Increase the speed, add 2 teaspoons of sugar and whisk for another 2 to 3 minutes. Increase the speed again to the fastest setting and add the last 2 teaspoons of sugar. Whisk until stiff peaks have formed, another 2 to 3 minutes.

3. In a saucepan, whisk the remaining ¾ cup sugar with the water and heat until the syrup comes to a simmer. Continue to simmer for 1 minute. If you are using a thermometer, the temperature should reach between 230°F (110°C) and 244°F (118°C).

4. Remove the syrup from the heat and slowly pour it into the egg whites while whisking them on high speed. Scrape down the edges of the bowl if necessary and whisk until all the syrup is well combined and the meringue is very glossy. Continue to beat the meringue on medium speed for another 5 minutes, this will give the egg whites enough time to cool down. Add the remaining half of the egg whites and beat again for another minute at medium speed to combine.

5. Replace the wire whisk on the stand mixer with the paddle attachment. Add the sifted almond powder mixture to the bowl and combine on low speed for 20 seconds. Scrape down the edges of the bowl and run again on low speed for another 20 seconds. The batter should be well blended but should not be over mixed.

6. Using a spatula, remove the mixture and place it in a pastry bag fitted with a 1A pastry tip.

7. Line three baking sheets with either silicone baking mats or parchment paper. Hold the pastry bag in a vertical position to pipe the macarons. Pipe the macarons at 1.5 to 2 inches in diameter and leave 2 inches in between each macaron. Each baking tray should easily hold 16 macaron shells, for a total of 48.

8. Once finished piping, grab your baking sheet with one hand and tap the bottom with the other hand. This will help flatten out the macaron shells so they don't over rise. Place a few rosemary leaves or small bits of the sprigs on top of half of the macaron shells and allow the shells to rest on their baking sheets for 30 minutes, until they form a thin skin. Preheat your oven to 300°F (150°C). Bake the macarons for 13 to 14 minutes. Remove the macaron shells from the oven and allow them to cool completely.

9. While the macarons are cooling prepare the chocolate ganache filling. Place the chocolate chunks in a heat safe bowl. Bring the milk to a boil. Pour the milk over the chocolate chunks. Allow to rest for 1 minute, then whisk the chocolate and milk together until a ganache forms. If the ganache is too liquid, allow the filling to harden in the refrigerator until a soft yet spreadable texture forms. Remove the filling from the refrigerator and allow to come to room temperature before filling the macaron shells.

10. Carefully unstick the macarons from the baking sheet using a thin knife. Turn half of the shells over—preferably the shells that are not topped with rosemary—so their bottom side is face up. Fill these shells with a teaspoon of the chocolate ganache and a sprinkling of rosemary leaves. Place the other half of the macaron shells on top of the ganache-filled shells to form 24 small sandwiches. Place the macarons in the refrigerator on an uncovered baking sheet overnight. Allow to come to room temperature 30 minutes before serving. Store the macarons in an airtight container in the refrigerator or freezer.

Chocolate Hazelnut Spread

Makes: Three 10-ounce
(280 g) jars
Preparation time: 10 minutes
Cooling time: 1 hour and
15 minutes
Cooking time: 11 to 13 minutes

5 cups (710 g) hazelnuts 600 g
1⅓ cups (264 g) sugar
¼ cup (57 ml) water
17 ounces (482 g)
  dark chocolate
2 to 3 tablespoons olive
  oil, as needed

This recipe is without all the added fats and oils of the iconic spread. It may take a little time and patience to make, but it's worth it. I love gifting this spread in jars—including one to myself of course! Aside from crêpes, pancakes, and toast (with a few banana slices on top), you can also spread it into leftover croissants when making Chocolate-Almond-Buckwheat Croissants (page 234).

1. Preheat the oven to 325°F (160°C). Spread the hazelnuts on two baking sheets. Place in the oven and roast for 12 minutes. Let the hazelnuts cool completely, about 45 minutes.

2. In a small saucepan, heat the sugar and water together. When the sugar starts to melt, whisk it vigorously. After a few minutes, the mixture will start to harden, don't worry, this is normal. At this point, replace the whisk with a wooden spoon, otherwise the sugar will harden in the center of the whisk. Keep stirring as the hardened mass begins to melt and turn golden. Once it is completely melted, carefully pour it onto a parchment-lined baking sheet. Let cool completely for about 30 minutes, then break into large caramel-like pieces.

3. Place the hazelnuts and caramel pieces in a blender or food processor (you will need one with enough power to handle these tougher ingredients). Start blending, pausing to scrape down the sides. As you blend, the mixture will heat up, so take breaks to avoid overheating. If you have a kitchen thermometer, use it: the temperature should not exceed 113°F (45°C). Allow to cool before starting the next step.

4. Melt the chocolate in a double boiler. Once it is completely melted, remove it from the heat. Allow to cool just enough to keep the chocolate stirrable. Pour the chocolate over the hazelnut mixture in the blender and begin blending again on low speed. Increase the speed if necessary until the mixture is smooth and almost liquid. Continue to control the temperature, if it exceeds 113°F (45°C), then pause for 30 minutes. Once you've added the chocolate, the trick is to go slow so you don't overheat the spread, or it will lose its ability to be spread. If this happens, let the mixture cool completely and blend it again, adding 2 to 3 tablespoons of olive oil if necessary.

5. Once the texture of the spread is to your liking (either crunchy or completely smooth), divide the spread into three airtight containers or jars. You can store the spread for up to 3 weeks at room temperature. If the spread seems too liquid, refrigerate overnight (this will have a hardening effect) and then store at room temperature.

Strawberry Rosé Spritzer

Serves: 2 to 4
Preparation time: 5 minutes

1 cup (167 g) red berries
(strawberries, raspberries,
cherries . . .), plus more
for serving
2 cups (480 ml) sparkling water
3 tablespoons lemon juice
2 tablespoons sugar
1 teaspoon freshly grated ginger
2 cups (480 ml) rosé
Ice cubes

My boyfriend's family recently traded in their city home and bought a rustic house in the South of France, near the border with Spain. It's a hot corner of France. Supposedly the hottest village in France is just two towns away. We use this as a reason (and sometimes an excuse) to finish the day in the garden with an aperitif. This drink started off very innocent, but then one evening when we were short on sparkling water but quite well stocked in rosé, the idea for this spritzer came about. Although not very common, there is a French tradition of mixing rosé with sparkling water, and surprisingly it comes from the same region as the rustic house where we first tried it.

1. Refrigerate the berries and the sparkling water for at least 1 hour before preparing this recipe. Place the berries in a blender along with the lemon juice, sugar, and ginger. Blend until smooth, about 30 seconds. Pour the fruit puree into a pitcher and add the sparkling water and rosé; stir gently. Serve with ice cubes and a little extra fruit.
2. If you keep the spritzer in a resealable bottle or container, it will keep for 24 hours in the fridge.

Acknowledgments

To the most supportive, important, and inspiring family, near and far. Thank you especially to my daughters; thank you for being there to help flip the crêpes, pipe out the macarons, and scramble the eggs. Thank you as well for the occasional French grammar corrections, mostly done with good intention and only minimal mocking, and for your understanding when I have to work over the weekends. Your unconditional love, curiosity, and generosity inspires and guides me.

To Christoph, thank you for enduring my extra workload and when I take forever at the market. Thank you for your point of view, whether behind a camera or when I'm recipe testing—and for making me your special eggs and potatoes with mayonnaise when I need a night off from cooking. Life tastes better with you.

To my parents and sister, thank you for your unconditional support no matter where I am. I am so very grateful.

To my friends and neighbors, thank you for your encouragement and opening the doors to your homes and to mine: Jaimee, Fem, Catherine, Karolina, Lisa, Isis, Stephanie, Orly, Amanda, Claire, Alex, Amelie, the Dufoix family. And a very special thank you to some of my earliest and dearest Paris friends: Julie and Onna.

And to my friends who lent me their kitchens, helped me find just the right vegetables, or took me out foraging in Brittany: Celine, Camille, Marie-Pierre, Aurelie and François, Judith, Marianne, Maud, La Fromagerie in Arles, and the entire Schwaiger family.

Thank you to the teams of the restaurants and kitchens where I have been a resident chef: Les Martyrs, La Tresorerie, Provisions Marseille, and Aube. Thank you for your trust and for providing me with the tools and produce, and for giving my cooking a sense of place and home in France.

To my editors at *Elle* magazine in France, thank you for giving me the opportunity to share my recipes with such a large audience, a truly humbling experience.

To the wonderful team at Le Creuset, and to Helene at North Communication, thank you for your confidence in my projects on both sides of the Atlantic. To Aurelie at Nathalie Lavirotte and to KitchenAid, thank you for following my dreams from Michigan to Paris.

To my agent Sarah at David Black, thank you for your thoughtfulness, support, and wise comments; for hearing out my brainstorms and for nudging me when I needed to be nudged.

To my attentive editors, Isabel and Ann, thank you for your patience and your careful eye; and to the whole team at Countryman and W. W. Norton books, from the marketing and sales to the design.

Index

Note: Page references in *italics* indicate photographs.